WEIRD ONTARIO LAWS

Strange, Bizarre, Wacky & Absurd

A.H. Jackson

BLUE
BIKE
BOOKS

The Publisher: Blue Bike Books
Website: www.bluebikebooks.com

Library and Archives Canada Cataloguing in Publication

Jackson, A.H., 1944–
  Weird Ontario laws / A.H. Jackson.
  Roger Garcia, illustrator.

ISBN-13: 978-1-926700-03-8

  1. Law—Ontario—Humor. 2. Law—Canada—Popular works.
I. Title.

K184.7.C2J32 2011   349.71302'07   C2010-907626-5

Project Director: Nicholle Carrière
Project Editor: Carla MacKay
Cover Image: Roger Garcia
Illustrations: Roger Garcia, Patrick Hènaff, Craig Howrie, Djordje Todorovic,
Peter Tyler, Roly Wood

We acknowledge the support of the Alberta Foundation for the Arts for
our publishing program.

We acknowledge the financial s upport of the Government of Canada
through the Canada Book Fund (CBF) for our publishing activities.

PC: P1

DEDICATION

To the Toronto Public Library, especially the hard-working staff in its Reference and Deer Park branches.

ACKNOWLEDGEMENTS

Kudos once again to the Toronto Public Library, particularly the Deer Park Branch, for so quickly supplying the tons of legal verbiage from which I extracted the shiny bits. A heartfelt thanks to the folks at Blue Bike as well, for allowing me "freedom of expression," including the odd rant, and to my editor Carla MacKay, who undangles my participles and perceives my intentions like a mind reader. I also give credit to my wife, M, who puts up with me writing before the birds are up and my noisy coffee making.

CONTENTS

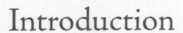

Introduction

Giving money and power to government is like giving whiskey and car keys to teenage boys.

–P.J. O'Rourke, political satirist

THE FIRST LAWS OF THE LAND

In the Beginning

In order to understand how certain Ontario laws transcend common sense and become "weird" requires a brief history lesson. Have patience, because to make head or tail of Ontario and its laws, it's beneficial to first know how the province got into the pickle called modern times. In Ontario's early years, and before it even went by its current name, southern Ontario (the area not owned by the Hudson's Bay Company) was part of Québec, and was a no-man's-land full of dark forests populated by a few hundred French trappers and thousands of warring First Nations, including the Huron and Iroquois. It could be said that these tribes laid down the first law of this land: we catch, we kill, and we do it most unpleasantly. Sure, that seems like an odd credo nowadays, but in 1645, to die miserably was almost expected because most of the fools that journeyed west from Fort Frontenac (now Kingston) into Ontario simply disappeared. A few years later, however, around 1649, the Iroquois attained the upper hand in that aforementioned inter-tribal fracas, thanks to firearms procured from the Dutch. As a result, folks near and far who wanted to try their hand at commerce in the area saw their chances of survival increase considerably because, at the time, an Iroquois not at war was an Iroquois with trade on his mind.

The Iroquois trapped beaver and other fur-bearing creatures, and traded their pelts to itinerant woodsmen who began their careers transporting furs for the Hudson's Bay Company. These *coureurs de bois*, or "runners of the woods," often literally played with fire, because in addition to trinkets like mirrors and beads, the trade goods that were most in demand were such volatile items as firearms, gunpowder and cheap whiskey. Not surprisingly, trading expeditions often turned ugly, and the runners needed places to hide (and defend themselves) while their customers sobered up or ran out of gunpowder. For this purpose, the runners constructed small forts, and even though the French military had absolutely no interest in the vast, never-ending land of lakes and forests that was southern Ontario, commerce—even that of a dubious nature—needed protection, so reluctant French authorities dispatched troops to occupy the runners' forts. A weird martial law began to govern the land, and the *coureurs de bois*, the men who drove the engine that brought wealth from the forests out into the pockets of Québec seigneurs and the financial backers of the lucrative fur trade, were untouchable by military law for any crimes committed, save stealing government property. In other words, the rape, murder and pillage of Aboriginals by both soldiers and runners was ignored, but

stealing a soldier's socks—a hot commodity in the wild—
resulted in the culprit, regardless of nationality, being shot or
strung up in the nearest tree. The Iroquois, understandably
put off by the French since the kidnapping of their chief
in 1535–36 by Jacques Cartier, responded to the stringing-up
regulation by reinstating their first law of the land: we catch,
we kill, and we do it most unpleasantly. Exempt from this
law, however, were the *coureurs de bois*, who the Iroquois
needed to supply the trade goods. A funny state of affairs
endured until 1756, when France and England went toe to
toe in a little altercation called the Seven Years' War. This was
a call to arms that quickly spread from Europe to the New
World, and it is known historically in North America as the
French and Indian War. What this meant for the wilds of
Ontario was that French military garrisons suddenly got the
full monty from the Iroquois, and ended up running for their
lives from every base except Fort Frontenac.

In 1758, however, Fort Frontenac was overrun by British and
Thirteen Colony troops, and it was destroyed by explosives.
The following year, Québec City fell, and in 1760, the New
France governor, Pierre François de Rigaud, Marquis de
Vaudreuil-Cavagnal, surrendered Montréal to the British.
English common law had arrived in New France—all hail
King George III!—which meant the end of French law. At
least, for three years it was end of French law, because
in 1763, King George issued a royal proclamation that was
designed to placate the French residents of Québec and assure
North American First Nations tribes of the sanctity of their
lands. In other words, Québec residents could keep their civil
law, while First Nations tribes were allowed access to all lands
west of the Appalachian Mountains. Of course, these agreements seemed fair to King George and his government, but
there were flies in both ointments. The Anglican Church (the
Church of England), was paramount in Québec at the time,
and it received tax support, but the Québec seigneurial

system, with its fiefs, contractual workers, duties and taxes, also continued, with the common folk governed by British common law. It was a weird mix that eventually caught the attention of North American First Nations bands because it was discovered that in the fine print of the Royal Proclamation of 1763, Britain was to be given leave to move the Appalachian Mountains' demarcation line westward if conditions were deemed appropriate. King George's proclamation also contained a caveat that made it illegal for First Nations peoples to sell their land to any agent not affiliated with the British government. Issued in English to people who could not read or speak the language, the King George Royal Proclamation of 1763 was Ontario's second weird law, and of the affected First Nations peoples, it was Pontiac, a war chief of the Ottawa band, who first smelled a rat. Thus ensued a massive uprising of many tribes, a "condition" the British considered appropriate for the movement of the demarcation line west to the Mississippi River. This was a 1774 action of British parliament called the Québec Act, and the decree created one province that stretched from the Atlantic Coast to the Ohio Valley. It also guaranteed residents of Québec their civil law, as well as established the first boundaries of Canada West, a.k.a. Ontario. Not that anyone cared—the new boundaries only offered more lakes, more dark forests and something called lake fever, a type of mosquito-vectored malaria that affected people around the Great Lakes region. Rampant lake fever goes a long way toward explaining why most Canadian First Nations bands were amenable to moving west of the Mississippi River demarcation line. Now, many First Nations claim they were cheated by the British, but back then, they were probably all smiles and chuckles over the white man's stupidity. One can almost hear the whispers: "There are no moose left, and they're going to be sick as dogs. Why would anyone want to live there?"

Why, indeed, and no one lived there again until 1783, the year the American Revolutionary War ran its course and Britain ceded all its colonies and lands to the victor, thereby creating a rush to Canada by colonists who were loyal to the Crown, a group of people otherwise known as United Empire Loyalists. These refugees headed north in droves, and as many as 50,000 arrived in Nova Scotia and in areas along the St. Lawrence River. Suddenly, people of English descent outnumbered the French, and the anglophones were not happy living under French law. In response, the British parliament passed the Constitutional Act of 1791, effectively splitting the province of Québec into Upper and Lower Canada.

The English naturally inhabited Upper Canada, while the French made do with Lower Canada. What was strange about this—at least, back then—was that what had been the butt end of Québec was now the top. Britain was, to say the least, eager to anglicize this vast area. The English authorities promptly sent 5000 Loyalist families west and equipped them with a tent, clothes for three years, food rations, one hoe, one axe, a few bags of seed, one musket for every five families and one plot of land selected by a draw from a hat. These people moved into the land called Canada West, or "Ontario," named as such after the largest lake in the area. Their immigration was a fortuitous move because without it, Ontario might have remained uninhabited for another century. Instead, down came the forests, up went the houses and the buildings and dams to run the gristmills, and the dreaded lake fever all but disappeared as the swamplands were drained. Hey! It wasn't such a bad place after all, and Britain owned a lot of it, thanks to the Royal Proclamation of 1763.

To facilitate more immigration, British authorities began to give away land in tracts of various sizes and locations, some of which was good for farming, some of which was mediocre and some of which was terrible. This action opened the door to speculators, particularly American United Empire Loyalists, who arrived bag and baggage, and with slaves. Plantations worked well in the South, so why not in Ontario? The province ended up with such a slave problem that it outlawed slavery in 1793, but, unfortunately, the legislation (the Act Against Slavery) put in place to (mostly) stop the practice failed to immediately halt the insidious endeavour.

The Act Against Slavery came from Upper Canada's first lieutenant-governor, John Graves Simcoe, and allowed farmers and plantation owners to keep existing slaves until they died, prohibited the buying of new slaves and provided freedom for the children of slaves at age 25. This quasi-solution lasted until 1819, when the Attorney General of Upper Canada outlawed the practice entirely. In Lower Canada and the Maritimes, however, slavery continued until 1834, when British parliament finally prohibited the keeping of slaves throughout the Commonwealth.

Stepping back into the late 18th century, Lieutenant-Governor Simcoe pretty much set the law of the land from 1792 to 1796. Supported by a nine-member legislative council and a 16-member legislative assembly mainly composed of the younger sons of English nobles, Simcoe issued many edicts, most of which were designed to prepare Upper Canada for war with the U.S. Simcoe's most notable decree was his decision to give payments to some First Nations tribes for lands confiscated under the Royal Proclamation of 1763. He moved these tribes into areas close to the boundary line, the 49th parallel, which was a border established by the 1783 Treaty of Paris that formally ended the American Revolutionary War and separated the newly declared American states from British Canada. This was considered by many to be a pointless edict because Britain already had claim to the lands, but Simcoe's actions, along with his compensation payments, were much appreciated by First Nations and eventually helped them stay loyal to the British in the brewing conflict with the Americans.

Invalided back to Britain in 1796 because of illness, Simcoe never saw the fruits of his relation-building efforts with the First Nations, which was unfortunate because the Six Nations, led by war chief Joseph Brant, was instrumental in the defence of Upper Canada during the American invasion of 1812. The Americans attacked, slapped the population around a bit, burned the government buildings in York (a.k.a. Toronto), and in 1814, were chased back across the border like errant schoolboys. Canada West had been ready for them, and it retaliated for the burning of York by invading the American capital of Washington and torching the government buildings. It was a tit-for-tat game that created hard feelings and a further separation of French, British and American neighbours. So much animosity existed that in 1818, a committee of British and American statesmen met and established an international boundary along the 49th parallel. Canada was beginning to take shape, but under a weird bijudicial system that included the French Civil Code of Lower Canada and British common law. In other words, Canada was one nation divisible under two laws that allowed the stage to eventually be set for the Québecois and other indigenous peoples to become separate and semi-separate entities within the Canadian constitution. At the time, though, one-half of the system, British common law, raised the curtain for Ontario's first land-registration act, because according to the English, if land was to be legally occupied, it needed to be deeded, and that required registration with the government in York.

Deeding, or the registration of title, needed the hand of a solicitor because in the British common-law system, solicitors did the paperwork, whereas barristers operated in the courts. In Ontario, however, there were simply not enough lawyers to fill all these positions. So, since Canada West was suffering from a shortage of legal eagles, the Law Society of Upper Canada decided that for a land registration or transfer, one lawyer could represent both vendor and buyer. The legality of two parties sharing one lawyer existed in Ontario until 2008, when, under pressure by the Law Society to create more employment for a surplus of lawyers, the shared-counsel law was repealed and replaced by Bill 152, which states that each party in a land registration or transfer must employ separate counsel.

This is just one example of a long-time legal inaction that hints at other kinds of now-stagnant laws that governed Ontario residents in the early days—laws that were promulgated by self-interested groups who wanted to make money, most notably the lumber, mining and railroad industries, fraternal organizations and...the Hudson's Bay Company.

WE BELONGED TO RUPERT

HBC Rules

On May 2, 1670, the English king, Charles II, signed a decree that awarded all the lands in the Hudson Bay watershed to a trading group that included the Frenchmen Médard Chouart des Groseilliers and Pierre-Ésprit Radisson, the king's cousin, Prince Rupert of the Rhine, and several wealthy merchants and English noblemen. Called the Governor and Company of Adventurers of England, or the Hudson's Bay Company (HBC), the group was the outright owner of Canada's vast north, an area they called Rupert's Land after the company's royal benefactor and first governor, Prince Rupert, who was also a Freemason. The royal charter gave the HBC carte blanche to enact laws, prosecute offenders and set up fiefdoms that it called factories, which were ruled by a manager or "factor" in a system that mimicked the monarchy. Factors were dukes allied to the barons of the HBC who, of course, owed their allegiance to the Crown. The dukes weren't happy, though, to only operate within the Hudson Bay watershed.

The business of the HBC was beaver, and HBC factors began to interpret their territorial borders to mean beaver country—that is, everywhere. This assumption brought HBC factors into conflict with the French and an upstart trading company based in Montréal named the North West Company. The clash escalated into outright warfare, with each side arming local First Nations tribes to act as soldiers. But, oddly, neither faction was keen to occupy the southern areas of Ontario because weather and mosquitoes made the area inhospitable, lake fever was rampant and a loathsome biting insect called the blackfly made life there miserable. Around 1816, however,

HBC factors received orders from London, England, to clean out all the southern beaver and move operations north, so within two years, the once plentiful beaver was a rarity in the southernmost areas of Ontario.

In 1821, the HBC and the North West Company merged, and in addition to 173 HBC trading posts, the companies came into control of an area that covered almost five million square kilometres, including most of Ontario. The merger precipitated a frenzied harvest of beaver in northern Ontario as the company headed west, to where the buffalo roamed and the otter swam.

Big Brass Beaver Bucks

After the 1821 merger, the Hudson's Bay Company became a financial goldmine and was much its own country, even going so far as to mint currency, the big brass beaver buck. Valued at one beaver pelt, the brass token became the coin for half the country. In 1849, the company grew ever larger when the British parliament granted the HBC the rights to Vancouver Island. Rupert's Land completely covered Upper Canada, which encompassed northern Ontario, the North West Territory (the Northwest Territories) and most of what is now BC. In 1863, however, a French investment company with little interest in fur trading bought controlling interest in the HBC and leaked word it was amenable to the sale of Rupert's Land to Britain and Canada, but the price was to be high, payable in land and pounds sterling—no brass beaver bucks allowed. The agreed price for what practically amounted to half of Canada was £300,000 (approximately $475,000), one-twentieth of the region's fertile lands, which were to be open for future settlement, and all the territories in which the HBC had established trading posts.

Ontario's Little Emperor

To momentarily go back a few years, enter Sir George Simpson, a man who rose through the ranks of the HBC to become governor-in-chief of Rupert's Land in 1820. Simpson took over what had become a less-than-profitable venture and got it back on the track toward big money. Under his steadying hand, Rupert's Land grew to include the entire northwest of Canada, the Alaska Panhandle and Oregon Country down to the 45th parallel. Simpson ruled Rupert's Land with all the power of an Old World monarch; he made laws, enforced them and brooked no interference from anyone. As one Hudson's Bay factor wrote of Simpson:

> *In no colony subject to the British Crown is there to be found an authority so despotic as is at this day exercised in the mercantile Colony of Rupert's Land; and authority combining the despotism of military rule with the strict surveillance and mean parsimony of the avaricious trade. From Labrador to Nootka Sound the unchecked, uncontrolled will of a single individual gives law to the land… Clothed with a power so unlimited, it is not to be wondered at that a man who rose from a humble situation should in the end forget what he was and play the tyrant.*

Simpson ruled most of Canada and all of northern Ontario for over 40 years, and he was instrumental in the exploration and charting of a large part of his domain.

In 1857, a select committee of the British House of Commons that was investigating all facets of the HBC's activities in Canada called Simpson as a witness. Simpson had a vested interest in maintaining the status quo on his land, and he testified that Rupert's Land was unsatisfactory for settlement, but in the end, the committee dismissed Simpson's opinions and recommended the annexation of Red River country and Saskatchewan to Canada. The problem now was that the country lacked the resources to purchase a railway to connect all its parts, and the British House of Commons' recommendation hung in limbo for another decade.

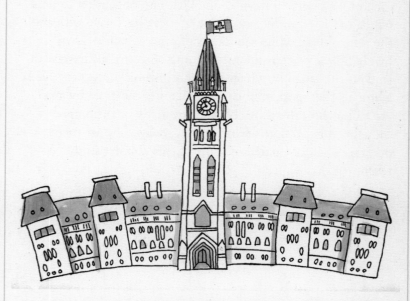

Things started to change on July 1, 1867, when, under the British North America Act, Canada became a Dominion in the British Commonwealth, with Britain maintaining control of legislation and foreign policy until 1949. However, at that time, the HBC still owned half of Canada, and the funds had not yet been raised to pay the French investors who had Rupert's Land up for sale. Canada had a babysitter and an unwanted beaver buck, but it also had the opportunity to create a federal government structure that included its own House of Commons, Senate and judicial and tax system, as well as the power to create new provinces and territories.

Then, in 1870, Canada finally purchased Rupert's Land, and the HBC took on a new identity, as it began selling farms and merchandise to new settlers. In 1871, the federal government began construction of the Canadian Pacific Railway, and the HBC followed it, shipping goods and assisting the fledgling settlements that sprang up almost overnight. These settlements became villages, and then incorporated towns, each of which had a town council with an obligation to pass regulatory laws, or bylaws. Some of these laws have withstood the test of time, while thousands of others, such as laws involving the placement and cleaning of spittoons, have withered on the vine like winter grapes. However, unless repealed, a process that most municipalities ignore, these old bylaws are still technically valid. Nowadays, many of them are thought to be strange or dumb, but, really, they are merely oddities when compared to some of this country's more recent legislations!

WEIRD LAWS TO GET YOU STARTED

Beavertown

HBC factors did much of the mapping of the North Country, and although they wielded a wicked pencil, their reason for being there in the first place was never far from their minds because over 1000 places on their map of Canada included the word "beaver," and approximately half of those towns were in Ontario.

What's that Smell?
According to HBC law, only two types of beaver pelts could be exchanged for brass beaver bucks—the standard stretched and cured dry pelt, and the disgustingly rank "greasy pelt." Greasy pelts, or "greasers," were used by Aboriginal trappers and company voyageurs as winter coats. Worn with the fur on the inside, motion removed the long hairs from the pelts, and the wearer's body supplied the oil and sweat to keep the fur supple—a process that was eventually ideal for the manufacture of felt hats.

A Gift Fit for a Queen

A stipulation in the original HBC royal charter from 1670 says two elk skins and two black beaver pelts are to be given to any visiting royalty. The last monarch to receive a variation of this gift was Queen Elizabeth II, who received two live beavers that she donated to the Winnipeg Zoo. Such a gift is obviously no longer officially expected, but this ritual has spawned an urban legend that predicts the demise of the HBC should the ceremonial rent not be paid. All hooey— or is it? Rumour has it that HBC store managers maintain a stock of elk-skin blankets and black beaver pelts should royalty arrive unexpectedly.

Trapper School

Today, Ontario fur trappers have to successfully complete the Fur Harvest, Fur Management and Conservation course before they can obtain a trapper's licence from the Ministry of Natural Resources. Licensees are assigned the species they're allowed to trap, the numbers they're permitted to kill and the dates on which the animals can be caught. All of these regulations are based on historical data gathered and compiled by the ministry. With respect to the beaver, however, it's a requirement of the licence that 75 percent of a licensee's quota be harvested in order to prevent overpopulation.

Westward, Ho!

The Rupert's Land Act of 1868 legislated the purchase of the HBC holdings in North America, and in 1869, the HBC signed a Deed of Surrender that gave the company 2.5 million acres (1 million hectares) of fertile western prairie lands. In 1880, when the Canadian Pacific Railway was still under construction, the HBC began selling tracts of this land to immigrant settlers, land speculators and Ontario farmers.

Fraternal Law

Freemasonry is not a secret society. Everybody knows that the Masonic fraternity exists and no effort is made to hide the fact. It is only the wisdom of Freemasonry which is hidden, not because it is subtle, but because it is simple. Its secret is profound; not obscure.

—Author unknown

FREEMASONS AND ORANGEMEN

Shake on It

It's not legislation, nor is it recorded for posterity, but in Ontario's early years, it was often the prime legal and financial directive. If you wanted to play with the big boys, you had to toe the mark, stand on the square, be on the level and get the third degree of Freemasonry.

The Masonic Law of Ontario

Brotherhood, relief and truth are the main tenets of Freemasonry, and during the American Revolutionary War, which lasted from 1775 to 1783, the leaders of the opposing forces, General George Washington and General Charles Cornwallis, were Freemasons, along with most of their officer corps. Additionally, John Graves Simcoe, a commander of the Queen's Rangers during the war, was also, as previously mentioned, a Freemason. After the war's conclusion, Simcoe was transferred to Upper Canada as a lieutenant-governor, and ended up in Niagara. He wasn't shy about giving preference to his kinsmen, and if someone happened to be a Masonic brother, he was generous to a fault, at times tripling or quadrupling land grants to these applicants. The members of Simcoe's Upper Canada legislative assemblies were also lodge brothers, as were most of his military officers and the millers and brewers he encouraged to emigrate from England.

When Simcoe moved the seat of government from Niagara to York, he established a new lodge, leaving behind the Niagara membership as a form of quasi-municipal government. In 1796, Simcoe took ill, sold off the 12,000 acres (4856 hectares) of Ontario land he had accumulated and returned to England, but his successors, all Freemasons, continued on in his place.

The Masonic brotherhood as law went on unabated even after Confederation in 1867, when Freemason Sir John A. Macdonald arranged the investiture of fellow Mason, John Sandfield Macdonald, to the office of premier of Ontario. However, in 1873, Sir John A. Macdonald let himself be influenced one too many times by the industrialist (and Freemason, of course!) Sir Hugh Allan. As a result, Macdonald's ruling Conservative Party was caught up in the infamous Pacific Scandal, which was a railway payola faux-pas that caused the Conservatives to lose the next election to the Reformers (Liberals). A lesson learned, the Masonic order confined government ear-bending to its lodges, but even that has been essentially free of hardship because nearly all of Ontario's premiers have been "on the level," as have most historically important Ontario financial and political luminaries.

The public might not realize it, but Freemasons have exerted their influence over national and regional police services as well, including the formation of the Royal Canadian Mounted Police (RCMP), the federal police service that still carries Masonic emblems on its uniform's shoulder patches and also continues to field an RCMP Masonic drill team that performs at lodge functions.

The Orange Order Societies

In Upper Canada, wealthy merchants, military officers and politicians were often members of the Freemasonry, while the common folk and farmers were instead part of the Irish-inspired Orange Order societies. There was little difference between the two societies because Orangemen practiced (and still practice) many of the rituals associated with Freemasonry. However, a person would have had to be "on the level" and a high-degree Freemason to know the truth.

In 1884, a bid to incorporate the Orange Order into the Canadian House of Commons failed after a fiery denouncement speech by Liberal leader Edward Blake, and this ended up as an action that doomed the Liberals at the polls for many years. Orangemen voters abandoned any Liberal sympathies, and, for the most part, sided with the Conservative Party, quickly becoming the backbone of that organization, especially in Ontario. The Orange Order grew to be powerful, indeed. Take, for instance, the infamous "circus riot" of 1885, wherein Toronto firemen, retaliating against tavern violence visited upon two of their fellows by circus clowns, burned down the tents of the clowns' itinerant circus. That the firemen escaped punishment by the courts because the attending police refused to identify them prompted Toronto's leading newspaper, the *Globe and Mail*, to print the following: "There are three classes in the city which thoroughly understand one another as hale fellows well met—the innkeeper, the fireman, and the police. These classes are fed by the Orange Order."

Additionally, since most judges and justices of the peace from the late 1800s were recruited or appointed by the localities served by their courts, a homeboy mentality often affected their decisions, and because most men in these positions were either Freemasons or Orangemen, Ontario law remained lopsided well into the 20th century. Relief, after all, is a main tenet of Freemasonry, and members are obliged to "relieve" a fellow Mason of their burden, even if it happens to be a legal one. Freemasons have secret methods of identifying themselves to other brothers whom they have never met, and in early Ontario courts, these methods could often work legal magic.

Chinese Freemasonry
In 1885, Canada imposed a $50 head tax on Chinese immigrants, and in 1903, the head tax was bumped up to $500, an amount that effectively stopped the reunification of Chinese men with their families who couldn't afford to immigrate to Canada as well. China has a long history of secret societies, some of which have tenets similar to those of the Freemasons, and this is where the marooned Chinese turned for fraternity and benevolence. Chinese Freemasonry lodges are now found in all of Canada's major cities, and although no connection to mainstream Freemasonry is claimed, a rose is a rose is a rose. Hong Kong and Shanghai are also active lodge cities, with the latter being home to the Grand Lodge of China.

Crime
and
Punishment

I shall send up your case for a new trial—
by your Maker.

–Judge Charles Roleau, while sentencing
a murderer during the late 19th century

THE LONG ARM OF THE LAW

Public Hangings

During the early 19th century in Ontario, there were no less than 120 crimes that were punishable by death. A death sentence meant a public hanging, a spectacle that was always well attended by the local citizenry. In 1865, however, the death penalty was restricted to those who were guilty of murder, rape or treason, thus saving 12-year-old boys from a neck stretching when they stole food or took a joyride on a neighbour's horse. Citizens waiting to see a good hanging now had to wait months instead of days, but, morbidly, that only increased the event's popularity. The times, though, they were a-changin', because it was four years later, in 1869, that Ontario saw its last public hanging. The unlucky man who suffered that fate was Patrick Whelan, who was convicted in the shooting of Ottawa politician and Father of Confederation, Thomas D'Arcy McGee. Afterward, Ontario moved its gallows into jail yards. People didn't want to give up their entertainment, though, and desperate souls were known to scale trees and sit on rooftops, just so they could see a condemned person die. It wasn't until the turn of the 20th century that Ontario jails moved their scaffolds inside.

Nasty Punishments

Besides hanging, old Ontario had many other unpleasant ways to punish legal transgressors. For petty crimes, a brand on the tongue or hand was common. In 1802, however, Ontario banned branding, except in cases of manslaughter, so, instead, public floggings became the new favourite form of punishment.

Floggings were usually 39 lashes with the infamous "cat o' nine tails," a multi-stranded whipping device. But, as would happen with hangings after 1869, flogging was removed from the public arena in 1830.

Stocks and the pillory, on the other hand, were not commonly used, but that didn't mean they weren't allowed, and certain magistrates held a preference for these particular brands of punishment. Stocks were squared timbers with two semicircular holes in the top and bottom that secured a prisoner's legs when the timbers closed and locked. Set in a public square, with his or her legs immobilized, a stocked prisoner was at the mercy of crowds but was at least still able to fend off eggs and rocks. Victims of the pillory weren't so lucky. It had holes for a prisoner's head, hands and feet, so the person was completely locked down and vulnerable.

Show Trials

Awing the public with pomp, circumstance and harsh sentences was a long-time favourite trick of British magistrates, and in 1814, the Attorney General of Upper Canada, John Beverley Robinson, decided to put on a show at a treason trial in southern Ontario. Robinson appointed to the trial three well-known and vainglorious magistrates—William Dummer Powell, Thomas Scott and William Campbell—and sent them off to Ancaster to conduct what is historically called the Ancaster "Bloody Assize."

In 1814, Ancaster, near Hamilton, was a small, rural hamlet mostly populated by U.S. immigrant settlers who had moved north after the War of 1812. The men accused in the treason trial were thought to be guilty of helping the U.S. forces during the war. And so it was that Powell, Scott and Campbell, dressed in regal robes trimmed in ermine, paraded into one of

Ancaster's churches and heard the testimony of 71 accused men. The "worships" released all but 17, and sentenced the unfortunates to be hanged. As if that wasn't enough, the judges also ordered that the bodies of the hanged men be drawn and quartered. After allowing a few days for their sentences to sufficiently scare the locals, the judges relented, pardoned nine of the 17 men and hung only eight, whose bodies were *not* drawn and quartered.

Ontario's Executioners

From 1890 until his death in 1912, Canada's official executioner was a man named John Radclive, and his most famous contribution to his profession was the "jerk 'em up" gallows. What this meant for the guilty party was that instead of being dropped through a trap door, a 350-pound (159-kilogram) weight was dropped, pulling the condemned off his feet and snapping his neck like a twig. Radclive officiated at the executions of 132 people, and eventually died in Toronto from excessive drinking.

In 1913, Arthur B. English, a British military executioner and nephew of John Ellis, England's official hangman, became the Dominion of Canada's top neck-stretcher. Using the alias Arthur Ellis, English dispatched over 600 people during his odious career, but his finesse with the rope betrayed him in 1935, when a weight miscalculation ripped a woman's head from her body and sent it flying into the audience. Prior to this incident, certain members of the public—relatives, reporters and weird friends of prison guards—were allowed inside jails to view executions, but the explosion of blood that came from this woman's neck put a quick end to that practice. Fired from his job, English died a pauper in 1938.

In 1987, a vote in the House of Commons put a permanent end to capital punishment in Canada, and the country retired its last official hangman, who used—what else?—the alias John Ellis.

Duelling in Ontario

In 1892, Section 71 of the Criminal Code of Canada prohibited duelling, an after-the-fact law inherited from the British that is still on the books. It is "after-the-fact" because there had not been an affair of honour in Ontario since 1833, when, in Perth, two law students, John Wilson and Robert Lyon, traded shots over a woman. Lyon died in the duel. Promptly charged with murder, Wilson was tried and acquitted, an expected outcome at the time because juries rarely convicted people when a duel was involved. Wilson actually married the woman he fought and killed for, and today, the town of Perth celebrates Ontario's last duel with an annual re-enactment of the event at Last Duel Park.

Duelling with pistols or swords was a common practice in Upper and Lower Canada, especially among the military, because the English Mutiny Act of 1689 required officers to defend their honour or else face dishonourable discharge from the service. The act was enforceable until 1844, when Queen Victoria got involved and had the law changed so that a court martial would try military duellists. Unfortunately, the Queen's involvement had little effect, because military juries refused to convict duellists. In 1847, however, British parliament passed a law that enabled survivors of duelling victims to sue for compensation. The practice of duelling soon came to a screeching halt.

The Ottawa Incident

In 1948, there was an incident in Ottawa between the consul general of the Dominican Republic and the ambassador of Argentina that almost eclipsed Perth's annual "last duel" re-enactment. At a cocktail party, while chatting with the Argentine ambassador's wife, the Dominican consul made light of the mysterious deaths of two dogs at Argentina's embassy. Incensed, the ambassador's wife lambasted the consul general with racially charged comments. She later ticked him off her party list, an action that further insulted the Dominican official. Angry, the consul general demanded satisfaction and sent his assistants, or "seconds," to the ambassador to choose weapons. Ontario newspapers had a field day, and since the duel was slated to take place at the Argentine embassy, police were powerless to intervene. Anticipation for the event reached a fever pitch in Ottawa, but a few days before the confrontation was to happen, Argentina recalled its ambassador, and the duel was no more.

Ontarians as Police and Prosecutors

The citizen's arrest section of the Ontario Criminal Code isn't weird, per se, but it does give the public the right to detain any person in breach of the peace. No more force than is reasonably necessary is to be employed before handing the perpetrator over to the police, and any or all lawsuits incurred are the sole responsibility of the arresting citizen. Besides being able to arrest others for drunkenness, commotions and fighting, citizens can also detain people for mischief, which is an obstruction by a person or persons of lawful use of property. Trespassing is another opportunity for a citizen's arrest. In breaking this law, an individual must contravene a notice not to trespass or disregard an owner's order to vacate the property.

Following a citizen's arrest, the police officer who arrives on scene has the option to refuse to charge the detainee, but the arresting citizen is allowed to privately charge the "perp," and bring the case before a court. Any Ontario resident may also be both arresting officer and prosecutor for those crimes.

The Poor Law

In the early 1890s, the Criminal Code of Canada was separate from Britain's but still followed England's legal precedents, even though some of them, such as the Poor Law, were archaic and class distinctive. The Poor Law originally dealt with idleness, and it allowed the jailing of beggars, vagrants and able-bodied people who refused work. The law was later expanded to include a host of infractions that most often involved the arrest of the poor—the operation of bawdy and gaming houses, public demonstrations, unlawful dismissals, tenant rights and child welfare. Many Ontario laws were rooted in the Poor Law and were used by prohibitionists against the use or practice of just about anything until the early 1980s, when an Ontario Superior Court put a stop to many aspects of the Poor Law. But yet, years later on June 15, 2000, police charged many of the participants in an anti-poverty demonstration outside Queen's Park with crimes rooted in the Poor Law, the most serious of which was "counselling"—that is, publicizing (by way of, say, a TV crew) a demonstration that comes under police attack. Legislations rooted in the Poor Law still remain on the books in Ontario, and it's unsettling that they can be resurrected by police or government at any time.

WEIRD LAWS ABOUT CRIME AND PUNISHMENT IN ONTARIO

A Dubious Landmark

On October 11, 1798, Toronto's first jail, a log structure located on the south side of King Street, opposite Toronto Street, was the site of Ontario's first public hanging. The unfortunate star of this event was a man named John Sullivan, who died because he forged a one-dollar note.

Get Outta Town!

In 1802, the Upper Canada legislature introduced the Banishment Act as a way to get rid of convicts. After being released from jail, a prisoner had eight days to remove himself from the province under the threat of death.

Constabular Conundrum

In 1823, Ontario was suffering from a shortage of constables. To solve the problem, magistrates turned tavern owners into constables because it was in bars that the majority of offences occurred. When Toronto was incorporated in 1834, the city had a population of 9200 and enjoyed the protection of 78 tavern cops, one for every 120 residents. In 1835, Toronto said goodbye to tavern police and hired five full-time constables, dropping the ratio to one constable for every 1800 residents. Tavern constables, however, remained a legal fixture in rural Ontario until 1887.

The Price of Justice

In 1997, criminal trials in Ontario courts required an average of 5.9 appearances before being resolved. By 2009, that number was 9.2 appearances, which cost taxpayers approximately $100 million.

You Have the Right...
In a 2010 decision, the Supreme Court of Canada refused to import American "Miranda Rights" into Canadian law. Miranda Rights denote the U.S. law that allows lawyers to be present during an interrogation by police. Ontarians arrested for crimes have a right to a phone call before going through an interrogation that may last up to 48 hours, after which they must either be charged or released.

Up in Smoke

The updated Smoke-Free Ontario Act of 2010 allowed the creation a new police service, the Ontario Smoke Police, who are inspectors hired by municipal health authorities to poke, pry and make sure that the 20 percent of adults who still smoke adhere to the law. The Smoke-Free act also lets police target private citizens who are thought to be purchasing contraband tobacco products. These people account for about 10 percent of Ontario's adult population.

Slavery in Ontario

For in reason, all government without the consent of the governed is the very definition of slavery.

—Jonathan Swift, English novelist

FORCED INTO LABOUR

The First Slaves

History attributes the founding of the first permanent settlement in Canada to Samuel de Champlain in 1605, but that is incorrect because although de Champlain was there at the time, the actual founder was Pierre du Gua, Sieur de Monts. Pierre employed a slave named Matthew de Costa, who was good with languages and served as an interpreter with local tribes. Was this the beginning of slavery in Canada?

At the end of the French regime in 1760, there were about 3500 slaves in Canada, and while a third were black, the majority were First Nations people known as Pawnees. Slavery continued in the country until its abolishment in 1834 with the enactment of the British Imperial Act, a law that prohibited both slavery and indentured servitude—though the latter continued in one form or another well into the 20th century.

Ontario's Slave Children

A lot of attention is paid to the history of slavery, especially that of black Africans, but little is said about its historical beginnings as indentured servitude. For instance, from the 15th century well into the 19th century, English farmers sold their children to the wealthy to work in the scullery or act as companions. Women sold themselves into servitude as housemaids or mothers' helpers, and men sold themselves as field hands. The indenture, or contract, ran until the amount paid in the initial transaction was compensated, and although servants had some legal rights, they were essentially the property of the contract holder and could be sold or traded as their owner saw fit.

In 1826, Robert Chambers, a London magistrate, commented to a parliamentary emigration committee that the city had too many children and they ought to be rounded up and sent to Canada as farm labourers. It was 1859 when his plan took effect, whereby Annie Macpherson, her sisters Rachel and Louisa and a friend named Maria Rye began sending London's unwanted youngsters to Niagara-on-the-Lake to be distributed to farms across the province. The women sent almost 15,000 children to Ontario, and all were indentured to repay their costs. The Macphersons' successful venture inspired dozens of organizations and individuals to gather waifs from the streets of London, and the most prominent of these people was Doctor Thomas John Barnardo. He sent over 30,000 children into Ontario's farm-servitude program. In total, from 1859 to 1929, over 100,000 children were forced into what practically amounted to slavery. This practice continued until the Great Depression caused the economic collapse of Ontario agriculture.

Ontario's Slave Labour Pools

The War Measures Act of 1914 was Canadian legislation that allowed the arrest, detainment and deportation of enemy aliens in the country who were deemed a threat to national security. In preparation for prisoners, the federal government constructed 24 internment camps across the country, with seven located in Ontario. World War I prisoners of war (POWs) were secured in these "concentration camps," but the majority of the inmates were Ontario civilians who were accused of acting in a suspicious manner, which usually meant that they were in an "undesirable" state of being or were poor and homeless. The prisoners were rented out to logging, mining, railway and road-construction companies, and when the war ended in 1918, the inmates' work program was deemed so successful that it ran for another two years.

In 1940, under imminent invasion from Nazi Germany, England once again brought the War Measures Act into play,

moving large numbers of German POWs to Canada and into various camps. In turn, Ontario began interning the POWs and renting them out for labour projects. The province even went a step further and set up satellite camps for POWs who weren't thought to be threats. These inmates were rented to private factories. In one such factory, the Toronto Brickworks (Canada's largest brick maker at the time), German prisoners did almost everything that required physical labour.

WEIRD LAWS ABOUT SLAVERY IN ONTARIO

Happy Birthday

During its early 19th-century heyday, Hamilton's Dundurn Castle, the home of one-time Ontario premier Sir Allan Napier MacNab, was the recipient of scrubbing, dusting and polishing by a legion of indentured children, some of whom also served as kitchen helpers. Hamilton now rents out the kitchen of Dundurn Castle for birthday parties that re-create the children's role as part of the help. In the castle today, kids bake cakes—and eat them, an indulgence that was denied the original children who lived there.

Back to the Grind

The Ontario Factories Act of 1884 improved some of the conditions in which children worked, including the enforcement of a maximum number of working hours. Seasonal exemptions, however, were granted to food canners who employed thousands of children in deplorable conditions, for minimal pay, over an eight- to 10-week grind.

Someone's Looking for You

An 1818 advertisement in the *Kingston Gazette*:

> *Five dollars reward—runaway from the subscriber on the night of 30 September, John White, an indentured apprentice to me, aged fifteen, is short and stout built, four feet six or seven inches high, pock marked, had on a black jacket and trousers. White took along a small boy by name of John Myer Blunt, aged about seven years, is fresh faced, has large eyes, had on large ribbed corduroy trousers, a new wool hat, is very light for his age, when he walks his toes turn in a little. White also took along*

Jonas Coffiter, a boy seven or eight years of age, freckled in face, very stout built, had on old striped flannel shirt and brown trousers. All the above boys have other clothes with them.

Any person that will return the above boys to their master, or lodge them in any jail in this district and gives the subscriber proper notice of it, shall be entitled to the above reward.

–Moses Carnahan, Adolphustown

Good Intentions
Gone Awry

There are so many lawyers with their hands in the till there isn't room for money.

–Howard Engel, Ontario crime novelist

FAULTY IS AS FAULTY DOES

Spittin' in the Spittoon

Time is the great dictator of law because as it marches on, legislations deemed worthwhile by one generation are inevitably considered strange by those in the future. During the 19th century, almost every adult male in Ontario chewed plug tobacco, a habit that required spitting, and to prevent sticky floors, spittoon bylaws were created. Since no gentleman wanted to spit in the presence of a lady, the spittoon bylaws went through amendments that excluded females from frequenting any establishment whose patrons included tobacco-spitting men. These restrictions meant women couldn't really go anywhere. Spittoon laws are what modern folk would call good intentions gone awry because what the regulations did was solidify a woman's place in the social fabric of 19th-century Ontario—and that place was at home.

Spending Like Drunken Sailors

The Balanced Budget Act of 1997 was legislation that ordered the Ontario government's executive council and minister of finance to prepare and table balanced fiscal budgets that included a reserve to pay down the provincial deficit. Flush after having just tabled four consecutive balanced budgets, which created surpluses and almost cleared the deficit, the Ontario Conservative government passed the Balanced Budget Act to prevent excessive future spending.

In 2003, a newly elected Liberal government repealed the act and began spending like drunken sailors. By 2010, Ontario's civil servant list had increased by 22 percent, and the deficit had ballooned to over $20 billion, which was a most irresponsible state of affairs for such a richly endowed province.

Provincial debt then ballooned to over $212 billion by the end of that year. Isn't it weird how we allow our governments to repeatedly overspend?

The Constant Prohibitionists

Drinking and driving laws, which are well-intentioned, are also gold mines for Ontario's police services, insurance companies, lawyers, charitable groups and, as of 2010, companies that manufacture and install ignition-interlock devices in vehicles. The collective of these groups form a legally sanctioned juggernaut that is ready to pounce on drivers who ignore the prime directive of not drinking and driving. But how much can a person safely drink to "blow under" on a Breathalyzer test? Well, there is no definable limit because it depends on a variety of factors that include weight, age, gender, stress level, metabolism and, unfortunately, the mood of the police. One or two drinks with a meal is usually okay, but finishing off a glass before leaving a party will cause a Breathalyzer to read higher because traces of alcohol still remain in the mouth. Rinsing with mouthwash or sucking on mints can also cause erroneous readings, as can the acetone in the blood of diabetics.

No Milk for Schmidt

The Ontario Milk Act of 1965 says it's illegal to sell or process unpasteurized raw milk. The fact that cheese will self-pasteurize while aging is completely ignored, and Ontario cheese consumers can still purchase imported raw milk cheese from Québec and Europe.

Dairy farmers in Ontario sell to the Ontario Milk Marketing Board (OMMB) through a quota system established by the Milk Act. The quantity of milk that a farmer's herd produced in 1965 is the quantity of milk the OMMB picks up from the farm. After 1965, Ontario farmers who wanted to produce more milk by expanding their herd had to buy an existing quota from another dairy farmer, and in 1992, for Durham dairy farmer Michael Schmidt, who wanted 40 more cows, that meant coming up with almost $1 million. Schmidt didn't have the million, but he had a good brain and figured out how to have his cake and eat it, too. Because the Milk Act allows the home consumption of raw milk, Schmidt simply sold shares in his herd, with each share entitling the owner to a percentage of the cows' raw milk.

The OMMB seemed willing to overlook Schmidt's scheme—that is, until the farmer made an error in judgment by allowing his operation to be featured in a 1994 documentary by the Canadian Broadcasting Corporation (CBC). Two days before the film's release, in response to a complaint by the OMMB, the Ontario government charged Schmidt with 19 counts of contravening the Milk Act by selling unpasteurized milk. The charges were dismissed, but that didn't stop the province from trying to get Schmidt again, and an appeal to a higher court was launched. In the meantime, Schmidt's farm was repeatedly vandalized, cows were killed, milk products were seized and his family lived under electronic surveillance. Schmidt received little help from the authorities, and he was eventually forced to sell most of his herd and farm in order to pay his legal bills. The freedom-loving farmer persevered, however, and in 2010, when Schmidt appeared in court charged with the same offence—again—the judge ruled in Schmidt's favour, a decision that will probably force the Ontario government to alter its laws regarding raw milk co-ops.

We've Got You Covered

Ontario's Compulsory Automobile Insurance Act of 1990 requires vehicles driven on public highways to carry adequate collision insurance. Sure, it was a boon for Ontario insurance companies, but it still made a lot of sense as a law. Unfortunately, since then, insurance companies in Ontario have been scammed by duplicitous claims so many times that, according to industry reports, almost 15 percent of paid premiums go to fraudsters. In 2009, the average claim disbursed by Ontario auto insurance companies was an astounding $34,858 (to compare, Alberta's average claim was $3689). Something weird is definitely going on....

An Electrical Fiasco

Perhaps a bit short on memory over the $38 billion in debt that was accumulated by Ontario Hydro before its financial meltdown in 1997, Dalton McGuinty's Liberals passed Bill 150, the

Green Energy and Green Economy Act, in 2009, an act that is principally aimed at facilitating the construction of renewable energy sources with or without the approval of municipal governments.

A bit of background information: the Ontario Power Authority (OPA) was formed as an agency of the Ontario government in 2004 as a temporary fix for the lack of investment and faith in the power system because of the Enron fiasco and the government's influence over the province's electricity prices. Canadian companies in the business of building generating plants were simply not interested in Ontario, and in the hope that guaranteed cash payments would attract national energy companies, the Ontario government formed the OPA to broker deals. The OPA is now the main player in Ontario's energy game, and since its inception, it has made deals worth more than $11 billion, with no end in sight. Its transactions are long-term, extremely expensive contracts for conventional and unconventional power generation that includes the use of coal, hydro, atomic, wind and solar power. Unfortunately, the OPA doesn't seem to pay much consideration to the rapid advance of new energy technologies. For instance, the U.S. buys electricity from Ontario via the power grid, but technological advances in drilling have created huge (and available) stocks of clean-burning natural gas that are sure to make the U.S. less amenable toward paying a premium for Ontario power. Will Ontario consumers and taxpayers will be on the hook for this difference in revenue? And if so, how big will that hook be?

As outlined in the Green Energy act, the OPA is now contracted to pay green energy companies, the solar and wind-turbine folks, a maximum of 80.2 cents per kilowatt hour. It will do this while also paying the huge, publicly owned Hydro One 3.5 cents per kilowatt hour, a price the present-day electricity bills of Ontario residents is based on.

Residents and municipalities that install rooftop solar panels will do well selling to the OPA, as they will get the 80.2 cents per kilowatt hour. Over 19,000 applications for solar-power installations have been submitted and are being processed, with more than 1000 projects already approved to feed surplus power into the grid. Towns such as Dryden are currently committing substantial sums to the construction of a solar park, while communities such as Brockville have already received approval and are poised to begin plastering hospital and school roofs with solar panels. Brockville is hoping for an income of $200,000 per annum from its grid feed, and as things stand, that is possible. Ontarians, however, should remember that Enbridge Inc., a natural gas company, has built a half-dozen wind farms and completed the world's largest solar-panel array in Sarnia. Enbridge also gets prime access to the power grid. In other words, people should be aware that big businesses trumping small producers hoping to recoup costs might, some day, put an end to the burgeoning solar-panel home-installation business in Ontario.

Many of the Green Energy act's strategies will never produce a kilowatt of profit because its raison d'être has all but collapsed along with U.S. cap-and-trade legislation (laws meant to sideline carbon-dioxide-producing utilities, primarily coal-fired generation, in favour of green energy). Some companies are sure to press forward, though, because, as mentioned, the Ontario government has promised to pay big money for green energy, as well as to allow green-minded companies preferential access to the electrical grid. The home generation of power, however, if largely denied access to the grid and saddled with exorbitant prices being billed, will translate into massive increases in traditional electricity costs to consumers, which, of course, will have everybody up in arms.

The Green Energy and Green Economy Act is turning into a mess, and citizens are right to fear for their tax dollars. The Ontario government has earmarked $87 billion for a 20-year project meant to increase the production of electricity in the province, with $33 billion slated for nuclear power, $14 billion for wind power, $9 billion for solar projects, almost $5 billion for new hydro-electric generation, $4 billion for biomass energy, $1.8 billion for natural gas plants, $9 billion for new transmission lines and towers and $12 billion for conservation programs. This money is likely being spent for what government studies have indicated will be a 15 percent rise in electricity consumption over the same 20-year period. This makes no sense when tax dollars could be better spent fixing what many see as a more pressing environmental problem—the pollution of rural water supplies by septic tanks.

A Big Surprise

Ontario residents who sign on to programs that substitute green energy for standard electrical power from the power grid expect to pay slightly more per kilowatt because going green is traditionally more expensive, thanks to new changes in technology. What they don't expect to see is a monthly charge for something called the Provincial Benefit. This fee is the difference between the spot market price of electricity and what the Ontario government pays to generating companies. It's a plus or minus charge factored into normal hydro bills, but it is also one that's listed separately on the bills of customers who have subscriptions with an electrical retailer that supplies cleaner, green energy. To people unaccustomed to this separate charge on their bills, paying slightly more per kilowatt hour can suddenly have them shouting, "Quick, Mary! Turn off the lights! They're burning our money faster than we can make it!"

Cough, Cough

Ontario is committed to ending coal-fired power generation and is spending billions of tax dollars to that end, claiming reduced carbon emissions and cleaner air for Ontarians via greener methods such as wind and solar power. Meanwhile, south of the border, about 30 new coal-fired plants pop up every year, and with prevailing winds wafting the emissions our way, people have to wonder if those billions could be better spent. Ontarians will be paying exorbitant prices for improved power and air quality, but how much change will they really see?

The Walmart Effect

In the mid-1990s, Ontario municipalities with shopping malls began falling over themselves to attract a Walmart store. And why not? Walmarts created new jobs, increased the tax base, attracted other big-box stores and, in those days, had some exoticism. But then the inevitable happened, and the Walmart and big-box stores began to take away business from smaller independent shops. Within approximately 10 years, people were angry and scared after seeing the closures of family businesses that had been around for years. Eventually, citizens retaliated. Guelph, for instance, waged a decade-long fight to keep Walmart out of its municipality, but was finally defeated by the Ontario Municipal Board and Walmart's deeper pockets. Other town councils, such as Gravenhurst's, are fighting the lure of big-box-store spending by revitalizing their downtowns and promoting shopping within them by removing parking meters and implementing extensive advertising programs. On the other hand, historical towns, such as Stratford, are still resisting, but Walmart is strong, and the sad fact is that community treasuries don't last forever.

Who Polices the Police?

Ontario's Independent Police Review Act of 2007 is legislation that allows an independent civilian review agency to deal with complaints against the police. It's a great idea—in theory. Unfortunately, the implementation of the act has been difficult because of the amount of red tape and politics involved. Ontario residents with complaints against the police are often advised by their legal counsel not to file because their cases are likely to be lost in bureaucracy and quickly become a waste of time and money. This is lamentable because even though the police are often society's protectors, there are, as everyone knows from the news, some incidents that definitely require the enforcement of edicts such as the Independent Police Review Act.

Butting Out in Ontario

To keep raising taxes on tobacco products so smokers will eventually quit is a simple idea. The difference between the lost revenue of quitters and the higher taxes is not supposed to cost the government a penny because the money brought in by people who are still buying cigarettes should balance out the decrease. But as the taxes are being raised in Ontario, what happens with cheap cigarettes from the U.S. that inevitably find their way across the border? In 1985, neither federal nor provincial legislators saw cigarette smuggling as a threat to their revenue because the rate at which it was happening seemed inconsequential, at 500,000 cartons bootlegged per year. However, by 1991, that number had jumped to almost 29 million cartons, which cost the government $500 million in lost income. Both the federal and provincial governments rescinded tobacco tax increases, and as a preventive measure meant to thwart manufacturers from shipping to smugglers, the federal government in Canada added an export tax on cigarettes. It didn't take long, however, for tobacco lovers to find a loophole, and that escape hatch existed right here in Ontario, on First Nations reserves.

First Nations reserves have become major purveyors of tobacco products, and the Ontario government is still losing millions in tax revenue.

Skirting Legalities

Ontario's Arbitration Act of 1991 provides a way to settle civil disputes outside the structured court system. It's a good idea because using trained arbitrators licensed by the Attorney General can be less intimidating and easier on the pocket-book when resolving disputes involving family law, divorce, marital separation, child protection and other domestic issues. Religious groups also agreed with the act's usefulness, and some Jewish communities set up tribunals called Beis Din, which adjudicated civil matters. Citing this as a precedent, Muslim groups are now demanding their own sharia tribu-nals, and this puts Ontario lawmakers in a hard place because Canada is committed to the rights of women under the

Canadian Charter of Rights and Freedoms, but sharia law is explicit in its denial of those rights. However, a group in Ontario, the Islamic Institute for Civil Justice, has since gained the right to hold tribunals (called Darul Qada) to settle business, marriage and family disputes. Is this the beginning of a slippery slope?

Forest Meddling
The Ontario Crown Forest Sustainability Act of 1994 was passed to assure the sustainability of the province's forests. The Ontario Ministry of Natural Resources oversees this act, along with about 40 regulations that pertain to every aspect of forest management, including wildlife. Just like everything else, the Crown Forest Sustainability Act seemed great at first. However, add in the provincial Assessment Act, the Environmental Bill of Rights and the Environmental Protection Act, along with the federal Constitution Act, Fisheries Act and Pest Control Products Act, and you have a jungle of red tape. Ontario's forestry industry, upon which many northern communities depend, has to deal with this mess every time it wants to do something. Compounding the difficulties of forestry are controversial issues such as the 2010 Environmental Protection Act and the Ontario Far North Act, which each set aside huge tracts of northern forest for use by migrating caribou. This decision will cost an estimated 3200 jobs, which could be the last straw for the many floundering Ontario forestry companies.

The End of Bright and Shiny Ontario

In Ontario schools, the word "Jesus" is practically verboten for fear of offending minority students—school-wide prayer, Christmas trees, nativity scenes and "O Canada" are shied away from and, in some cases, banned. In the mainstream population, "Merry Christmas" has become "Season's Greetings," and daring to question the activities of Israel can have someone branded as anti-Semitic or as a Holocaust denier. Called political correctness, it's all rooted in Ontario's Human Rights Code, which was passed in 1990. This well-meaning legislation created the Ontario Human Rights Tribunal, which is meant to curb physical acts of racial hatred, but its far-reaching legal powers and perceived influence by self-interest groups have affected the public's psychology, and the tribunal is often viewed as a club wielded by minorities. In 2010, hate crime charges escalated dramatically, with book fairs under police surveillance, and police services actively laying hate-crime charges adjunct to regular charges if victims were part of a minority group. On the other hand, it's no secret that minorities press charges for such things as perceived slurs, being fired and being evicted, and these actions have many Ontarians frightened of the fallout of associating negatively with minorities, even if it seems justified in certain situations. Is freedom of speech dead in this province?

The Competitive Edge

The Ontario Competition Act is designed to protect Ontarians from unfair corporate business practices, or price fixing. That the act fails on most accounts should be evident by the obvious similarity in prices charged for goods and services throughout most populous places in the province. It's frustrating how people are willing to put up with paying approximately the same price for gas, cable services, drugs, vehicles, utilities and beer, with the only relief found in the weekly flyers distributed by supermarkets (and even these are often advertise similarly discounted prices). Whatever happened to healthy competition?

Ontario's One-percent Law

The joint-and-several provisions of the Ontario Negligence Act allow courts to award shared punitive damages when two or more persons are found to be negligent. The problem, particularly in vehicle accidents, is that an individual's insurance coverage is often not enough to meet these amounts. However, when a negligence conviction is shared, the plaintiff can demand payment from whichever defendant has the deepest pockets—and more often than not, that is an Ontario municipality. For example, if judgment for a serious brain injury resulting from a vehicle accident is $7 million and is deemed to be one percent a driver's fault and 99 percent a municipality's for not clearing brush from in front of a stop sign, the driver's insurance will pay $1 million, while the municipality has to ante up the balance, hence the name "one-percent law."

In 2009, while overtaking another vehicle, an intoxicated driver in Ontario encountered gravel on the road, lost control and struck a tree. The driver was killed instantly, and his passenger sustained a serious brain injury—neither was wearing a seat belt. The municipality in which the accident occurred was included in the lawsuit because of its failure to put up signs indicating that roadwork was being done, and even though the driver was drunk and neither he nor his passenger was wearing a seat belt, judgment for the plaintiff was $9.39 million. The dead driver's insurance company paid out $2.67 million of that, and the municipality's insurance 1company covered the remaining $6.72 million. The municipality's insurance premiums doubled, and shortly afterward, the children's playground in the local park was dismantled for fear of lawsuits. The trepidation of being found liable has caused Ontario communities to cancel street parties and fireworks displays, and is the reason why some local swimming pools have been closed. Is it possible that the Ontario Negligence Act is, in itself, negligent?

Evil John Barleycorn

Once, during Prohibition, I was forced to live for days on nothing but food and water.

–W.C. Fields, comedian

DRINK UP!

Tavern Politics

In 1841, Ontario was awash in taverns. Every village and town had at least two, and major cities like London and Toronto had a bar on almost every street corner. In fact, in 1841, Toronto had 140 licensed taverns, one for every 52 residents, and almost every one of them was a vote-gathering factory for Tory politicians. On the other side, the opposition party, the Reformers (Liberals), aligned themselves with temperance unions until they were permanently mired in anti-alcohol politics, an unfortunate circumstance that later gave rise to prohibitions and the puritanical overview of how much liquor and beer was being consumed by Ontario residents.

No, Not the Drunkin' Act

The Dunkin Act of 1864 was legislation that allowed communities to enforce local prohibitions against the manufacture, import, sale and consumption of alcoholic beverages. Under this act, municipalities were allowed to hold "wet or dry" referendums. After Canada became a dominion in 1876, the Dunkin Act was changed to the Canada Temperance Act in 1878. This meant that the Parliament of Canada allowed municipalities to enter into prohibition schemes through plebiscites. People took this seriously for decades, and in 1904, the city of West Toronto, a.k.a. the Junction, voted to outlaw the sale of spirits, and even though it became part of Toronto in 1909, "West Toronto" stayed dry until 1998.

Cut Off…Almost

In 1916, World War I caused Ontarians to support "moral uplift," and 10,000 people descended on Queen's Park carrying an 825,000-name petition for the prohibition of alcoholic beverages. The premier of Ontario at the time, William H. Hearst, caved in to their demands, and his Conservative government legislated a complete ban on the sale of alcoholic beverages. From 1916 to 1927, Ontario, on the surface, appeared as dry as toast, except for drugstores—the law allowed the sale of alcohol for medicinal purposes. Additionally, soda fountains in drugstores popped up everywhere. Family physicians wrote prescriptions for "therapeutic" brandy or whiskey, and druggists filled those prescriptions, along with ice, mix and a place to imbibe.

The 1916 Ontario Temperance Act never really stopped Ontario's brewmasters, either, because they just kept on brewing beer and shipping it everywhere but inside their own province. It was perhaps this fact that led thirsty Ontarians to find a hole in the law—mail order. Residents simply sent orders with payments to out-of-province agents, say, in Québec, and those agents ordered the beer from whichever breweries customers specified, returning the receipts to the purchasers. Receipts in hand, Ontarians went to their breweries of choice and legally picked up the order for their agents.

Fear and Loathing at the LCBO

The Ontario Liquor Control Act of 1927 came hard on the heels of the 11-year-long liquor prohibition the province had just suffered through, and it walked a political tightrope between powerful temperance unions versus the citizens who wanted to have a legal drink without a hassle. The new act sanctioned the formation of a marketing and surveillance agency named the Liquor Control Board of Ontario (LCBO). It operated under the mandate of selling liquor and knowing exactly who was buying the product—and for what reason. From 1927 to 1962, anyone who wanted to buy alcohol in Ontario needed a permit book and was required to fill out a form before every purchase. Drunkards and those convicted of public intoxication had their liquor purchases tracked and were refused service at LCBO outlets, thanks to the infamous Interdiction List. Buying too much liquor or beer, or being the cause of a complaint from police or a neighbour was also problematic because these circumstances were reviewed by a judge who could order that a person's name be placed on the Interdiction List. Besides denial of service, blacklisted people weren't allowed to purchase liquor or beer for a period that usually lasted about 12 months.

In 1929, another alcohol-related prohibition list was created, and it was called, fittingly, the Prohibited List. Its roll call consisted of people who received public assistance. In addition to the Prohibited List and Interdiction List, the LCBO also monitored alcohol use through the hundreds of liquor inspectors who prowled drinking establishments to make sure Ontarians were indulging according to the rules. Last published in 1952, the dreaded Interdiction List suddenly became shorter that year when the LCBO, in either a fit of conscience or the realization that those on the list were also voters, removed the names of 7000 people.

However, even though the Interdiction List was no more, there were other lists of dubious distinction that were created by companies who had agreements to ship bootleg whiskey— no permits required—straight from the distillery into the homes of Ontario politicians from the 1950s to the mid-1970s. These were called "B Lists," and they were maintained by out-of-province liquor agents. The destruction of the B Lists was eventually initiated because they were considered to be political hot potatoes. Go figure.

Since the mid-1970s, the LCBO has become responsive to its customers and has spent millions constructing new stores and modernizing the older ones. You wouldn't, however, have to go far to find someone who still calls the organization a monopoly…

The Vino Scam

The Cellared in Canada wine tax that came into effect in 2010 was thought by many to be just another government cash grab, but consumers were eventually shocked to discover what some saw as corporate shenanigans in Ontario's wine country. The term "cellared in Canada" is what vintners use to refer to "value-priced" wines that are usually sold in larger-than-normal bottles and contain only 30 percent Ontario wine. What was surprising about this was the government admission that value-priced wines are where most of Ontario's grape crop winds up, mixed with cheap plonk produced from grapes grown in other countries, mainly the U.S.

To give a bit of background, in the early 1970s, the Ontario wine industry moved away from sherry and sweet Concord wine when the demand for French varietals soared.

Unable to satisfy consumer appetites, Ontario grape growers appealed to the Ministry of Consumer and Commercial Relations to allow vintners to import varietal grape juice until the necessary crops could be planted and grown. The ministry complied, and in 2001, changed the Wine Content Act of 1970 to permit a proportion of grapes grown outside Ontario to be used in the creation of wine in the province. However, what the trusting grape growers and the government never realized was that the U.S. juice imported by Ontario vintners was concentrated and could be reconstituted to five or six times the amount listed on a waybill. The legislation created to help vintners had been turned into a proper hoodwink by...vintners.

In short, the production of wine, liquor and beer creates rivers of money that are irresistible to many. During the fiscal year 2009, on net sales of $4.3 billion, the LCBO saw a profit of $1.41 billion, not including taxes collected. Of the taxes collected, $874 million went to provincial, federal and municipal governments. Bureaucratic agendas aside, one has to admit that the LCBO does have at least a few good qualities. As the world's largest buyer of wines and liquors, the LCBO is able to provide consumers with a huge selection that spans 60 countries, and it is especially good at importing fine wines. The LCBO is also a bulwark that helps to counter shoddy manufacturing practices because every year it conducts around 200,000 tests on some 11,000 of their listed products. Additionally, the LCBO protects Ontario from public drunkenness and underage drinking—in 2009, the LCBO's employees refused service to 2.6 million customers for being underage or intoxicated.

Dan's Unloved Skull

Showing how it can wield its power, in 2010, the LCBO decided not to list a favourite son's vodka because it was packaged inside a skull-shaped bottle. Dan Aykroyd's Crystal Head Vodka was not to be found in LCBO stores because, according to the board, the product's packaging might give people the wrong impression about drinking since the image created by the bottle's shape was more associated with poison and death than with liquor. The bottle is actually a work of art, and it bears a purposeful resemblance to the Mayan crystal skull discovered by English archaeologist F.A. Mitchell-Hedges that was left to his adopted daughter Anna Mitchell-Hedges, a long-time resident of London, Ontario. The LCBO's reach only extends so far, however, and prospective consumers who find this vodka interesting can circumvent the LCBO and purchase Dan's Crystal Head Vodka by contacting its distributor, Globefill.

WEIRD FACTS ABOUT ALCOHOL IN ONTARIO

Things that Go Boom in the Night

British soldiers serving in Canada during the 18th century were entitled to a daily ration of six pints of beer, but during times of war or huge construction projects, such as the building of the Rideau Canal, the standard ration also included a few tots of overproof navy rum. A tot is an eighth of a pint—almost two ounces (59 millilitres)—and that was considered "overproof," or 50 percent alcohol as opposed to the normal 40 percent. There's nothing like courage from the bottle! (An interesting note is how the British navy proofed their rum—it arrived in England from various Caribbean islands, and was then drained from barrels and mixed to a proper navy taste. Water was added to dilute the rum to a drinkable state, and the mixture was checked for proof. Proofing rum was accomplished by pouring a bit of the liquor over gunpowder and then setting it on fire. If the wet gunpowder burned, it was proof, if it went out after lighting, it was underproof, and if it exploded...overproof.)

Is that a Crock in your Pocket?

In 1864, the town of Carlton Place, a logging settlement west of Ottawa, bent to pressure from temperance groups and passed a novel bylaw that banned the sale of liquor in quantities of less than five gallons. In those days, whiskey came in crocks, and the motivation behind the bylaw was to make it difficult for loggers to conceal small amounts of alcohol from their supervisors. The bylaw worked for about a month, the time it took for purveyors of whiskey (general stores) to import a supply of small crocks and hip flasks. One year after it was passed, the bylaw was repealed.

Separated Sipping

Up until the early 1970s, licensees of taverns and beer halls were required by the Ontario government to provide sepa-rate facilities for "ladies and escorts." Men drank in one room, women and their dates in another, and never the twain shall meet.

Something Stinks
Additionally, in certain places, during certain times, such as in hotels and licensed establishments on Sundays in the 19th century, patrons were allowed to buy a drink, but only if they also purchased food. Enter the stale cheese sandwich. Thirsty patrons would buy their drinks, along with a day-old cheese sandwich that was meant to be conveniently passed on to another imbiber. Myriad prohibitionist groups promoted the "blue laws" that perpetuated the cult of the stale cheese sandwich, and as history shows, when prohibitionists nag, the government acts and citizens find a way around the law— in other words, a constant war of wills between electors and elected, and a weird state of affairs.

Money Makers

In Ontario, the Ministry of Consumer and Commercial Relations oversees the LCBO, the Liquor Licensing Board of Ontario (LLBO), the Ontario Racing Commission and the Ontario Lottery and Gaming Corporation. The billions pouring in from these agencies makes small potatoes of all the other legislated acts under this ministry's supervision, which include looking after marriages, burials, elevators and, yes, upholstered furniture.

Party Hearty
Closing time for bars in Ontario is 2:00 AM, but permits to serve private affairs until 4:00 AM are routinely given out by the LCBO. It must be nice to be able to afford a private function!

The Grapes Groweth

The Vintners Quality Alliance Act of 1999 is legislation meant to establish and maintain a French-style appellation-of-origin system for Ontario wines. Consumers now only have to look at a wine label to determine how their wine was made and from whose backyard cometh the sour grapes.

You Can't Miss It

The city of Sudbury rents municipally owned facilities for banquets and special occasions, but requires a standard message be posted that imbibers watch their Ps and Qs. According to the bylaw, the following note from the police service is to be tacked up at every exit: "The Greater Sudbury Police Service thanks you for helping to reduce impaired driving everywhere in Greater Sudbury and area. We look forward to personally thanking you at one of our spot checks for leaving this event a sober driver."

Travelling Amusement

In Ontario, residents can be tried as an adult at 14 years of age, drive a vehicle at 16, join the military at 17 and vote at 18, but they can't legally drink a beer until they're 19. In 1971, the drinking age in Ontario was actually lowered from 21 to 18, but was later bumped up one year because teenage drinkers were causing too many vehicle accidents and, thus, complaints from the public. Unfortunately (or perhaps fortunately, depending on who you're talking to), Ontario's provincial neighbours, Québec and Manitoba, have a drinking age of 18, and it doesn't take a genius to figure out why droves of 18-year-old Ontarians can be found out of province on weekends.

Blue
Laws

*Laws that attempt to refine the morality of Ontarians—
the sale of alcohol and tobacco, store closings on Sundays,
the banning of various recreational drugs and so on—are
called blue laws. Some historians claim this is so because
the laws originally came from England and were printed
on blue paper, but others believe the laws were labelled
"blue" as an insult to the aristocrat-heavy English parliament that ruled Canada.*

MORAL MANDATES

Slow Sundays

Lord's Day blue laws transformed Ontario's communities into ghost towns every Sunday until the 1980s. The mandatory closing of all but a few essential businesses created no reason for vehicles to be on the roads, and since the Lord's Day Act prohibited noise, lawn mowers were silent, hammering was unheard of and motorcycles were nowhere to be seen. Except for morning church bells and chirping birds, nothing could be heard but an eerie quiet that ruled the day. At least, it seems eerie now—back then it was just boring. But there are elements to miss—time spent with family, friends and, perhaps, fellow parishioners in lieu of just another day of leaf blowers, lawn mowers, traffic gridlock and grinding public transit, all of which creates a din that makes it pretty hard to hear birds singing.

You Minded Your Manners in Old Sudbury

In 1893, in Sudbury, the ringing of a bell for reasons other than announcing a church service was strictly verboten under the threat of a large fine. God-fearing Sudbury folk in the late 1800s also had to follow a litany of other municipal blue laws: stores were closed on Sundays, taverns shut their doors at midnight on Saturdays, swimming was not allowed unless wearing the "proper" attire, spitting or farting was prohibited in public and begging was not permitted without a licence. Interrupting a town council meeting was yet another no-no. This seems almost laughable now, but residents probably avoided those meetings in order to guarantee they kept their mouths shut. Unfortunately, this muffling of the public likely created further prime ground for more so-called morality laws to be passed.

Keep the Kids Quiet

The town of Pelham runs a summer day camp for local children that, among other things, introduces them to the area's natural wonders, of which there are plenty. Kids had better mind their Ps and Qs, however, because parents are required to sign a "behaviour contract" so unruly nippers can be tossed out of the program. Kudos to the Pelham town council for refusing to employ the overseer attitude that's been adopted by most of Ontario's municipal councils, and instead choosing to be at one with its community...ahem.

Zoom, Zoom, Ontario

An OPP officer leans into the window of a car he has pulled over for speeding and asks the driver for his licence.

"I don't have one, officer. I lost it for driving drunk."

The officer, a tad shocked, asks the driver for the car's registration.

"I don't have that, either. You see, I stole this car and murdered the driver. He's in the trunk."

Thoroughly shocked, the OPP officer retreats to his vehicle and calls his sergeant for backup.

The sergeant quickly arrives on the scene, and with his gun drawn, he warily approaches the vehicle and demands that the driver open the trunk. Finding it empty, the sergeant asks, "Is this your vehicle, sir?"

The driver nods and hands over his licence, registration and insurance certificate. The OPP sergeant looks perplexed, and says, "One of my men says you stole this car, murdered the owner and have no licence."

The driver replies, "Yeah, and along with all those lies, he probably said I was speeding, too."

PEDAL TO THE METAL

Not Exactly a Passing Fad

In the beginning of convenient cross-province transportation, railways ruled Ontario, and train stations were the hubs of town and village life in the 1700s and 1800s. Most featured simple dining areas for passengers awaiting the refuelling or watering of steam-driven locomotives, and from these establishments evolved hotels and restaurants within easy walking distance. Then, on April 12, 1898, everything changed when Colonel John Moodie Jr., of Hamilton, imported the first gasoline-engine-powered automobile into Ontario. Called the Winton, after its Cleveland, Ohio, manufacturer, and a "stink wagon" by local Hamiltonians because the poor quality of available gasoline created clouds of noxious fumes, it was considered a passing fad by most Ontario residents. It didn't take long, however, for the fad to spread, and anyone who could afford the luxury quickly headed south to the U.S. to purchase their very own stink wagon.

In 1904, Walkerville residents Gordon McGregor and his two brothers began turning out Ford Model C automobiles at their Walkerville Wagon Works factory, which had a first-year production of 107 vehicles priced at $1100 each. In 1909, the Ford Model T began rolling off the Walkerville assembly line with a debut production of 1200 cars priced at $850 apiece. By 1920, the brothers were cranking out almost 19,000 cars a year, and the price per vehicle had dropped to just $300. A scant 22 years after Colonel Moodie brought his auto into Hamilton, almost anyone could afford a car. Sales took off, and with paved roads like the one between Lakeshore Road in Toronto and Hamilton being created, it seemed like no better time to put the pedal to the metal.

However, with no speed limits, no right-of-way laws, no seat belts and no ambulances, absolute chaos ensued. It was only when vehicle registration topped 150,000 in 1930 that the provincial government began establishing and enforcing speed limits by putting cops on motorcycles.

But I Wasn't Driving!

Drinking and driving laws are part of both the Ontario Criminal Code and the Highway Traffic Act, but they are weirdly obtuse. Ontario residents know that driving with a blood alcohol level above 80 milligrams per 100 millilitres is a criminal offence, but what most don't know is that actually driving a vehicle is not a requirement for being charged. "Care and control" of an automobile is the bugaboo, and if the police find someone asleep in the front seat of a parked car, that person can be charged with "driving while under the influence" if they blow over 80. "But your honour, I wasn't driving. I was sleeping!"

Paddling Prohibited

Paddling a canoe while intoxicated in Ontario is also cause for loss of licence, for one year. "But your honour, I wasn't driving and I wasn't sleeping. I was paddling a canoe!"

Insulin Incident

And what if the offender happens to be a diabetic? Well, he or she has a chance to get off because acetone levels in their blood can skew Breathalyzer readings.

Busted for Breathing

Another section of Ontario drinking and driving laws requires drivers, asleep or not, diabetic or not, to provide police with a breath sample. Failure to do so is tantamount to a confession in court and will garner offenders the same punishment as a driving under the influence (DUI) conviction.

Beware of the Bottle

Unfortunately, for those between 16 and 21 years old, as of 2010, it became illegal for drivers who fall into this group to have any amount of alcohol in their systems. Apparently not satisfied with the traffic already coursing through the courts, the Ontario government now essentially warns young drivers that having one beer could cause their parents to face bankruptcy trying to save them from having a criminal record.

Traffic Ticket Pileup

In 1999, the Ontario provincial government rid itself of
having to dole out justice to municipal residents charged
with infractions under the Provincial Offences and Highway
Traffic acts by empowering individual communities to deal
with the charges instead. Coincidentally, between 1999
and 2010, the number of traffic tickets issued in many
cities and towns doubled, and the number of criminal
charges rose almost 20 percent, with court backlogs so large
that wait times for the hearing of a traffic case can now be
eight to 10 months. The province is trying to sort out the
mess and has kicked in millions of dollars for extra personnel,
but the legal logjam gets larger by the day. Residents should
be able to expect rational town and city councils, but is so
much money rolling in from the tickets that no one cares if
the legal process is completely deteriorating?

Fifty and Up

The "50 over" law is an amendment to the Ontario Highway Traffic Act that's primarily aimed at street and stunt racers, but it can still affect any driver caught speeding more than 50 kilometres per hour over the posted limit. Driving suspiciously is punishable under this law as well, and odd behaviour can include anything from wandering over the centreline, to speeding up to catch traffic, to standing on a motorcycle's pedals in order to cross railway tracks. In reality, though, "50 over" mostly affects rural drivers who are cruising back roads much faster than the posted speed limit. Therefore, if a driver is ripping along a road at 100 kilometres per hour, misses a sign that indicates it's time to slow down to 50 kilometres per hour and is pulled over by the police, that driver might face having both their car impounded and their licence suspended for seven days, as well as a fine of $2000 and possible legal costs. Since the law was implemented in 2007, fines have totalled over $10 million, with most "crimes scenes" located in rural areas.

No doubt about it, some dangerous street racers have been caught thanks to this law, but citizens should also consider the other statute that says a police seizure of private property without a trial is summary justice and contravenes Canada's Charter of Rights and Freedoms and the Constitution of Canada. If drivers are caught speeding at 50 kilometres per hour over the posted limit, should police officers be allowed take possession of their car and leave them stranded on the roadside?

WEIRD LAWS ABOUT DRIVING IN ONTARIO

Car Cacophony

In 1926, outside the U.S., Ontario had the highest per capita car ownership in the world. Toronto roads were so filled with "cars a-honking" that council enacted a "reckless walking" bylaw with accompanying fines in a futile effort to protect citizens from automobiles. It was chaos until 1927, when Ontario began licensing drivers, a decision that slowly brought an end to the era of cacophony and general public mayhem on Ontario's streets.

Horsing Around

In Ontario, a horse-drawn sleigh driven on a highway must have at least two bells attached to the horse to allow for ample warning. Failure to attach said bells carries a fine of five dollars.

Get Out of the Way

In Windsor, it is against the law to block a driveway with a vehicle for any purpose, and offenders are subject to a $110 fine.

The Need for Speed

About three hours northeast of Toronto sits Bancroft, and drivers who want to drastically exceed the speed limit can do so here in November at the town's Rally of the Tall Pines. Redlining is legal and is confined to a course that includes most of Bancroft's backcountry roads. Not for the faint of heart, the rally is open to any licensed driver who wants to experience the thrill of risking life, limb and car.

Insurance Uncertainties

In Ontario, insured automobiles lose their coverage when in the possession of mechanics and parking attendants. If these people damage an automobile and don't have business insurance that specifically covers the handling of vehicles, the owner of the vehicle is on the hook. Maybe you'll think twice about trusting your expensive vehicle to the next car-park attendant you come across.

Boarding Bylaw

Blind River's town council became so sick of fielding citizens' complaints about kids creating downtown havoc with skateboards that it passed a bylaw banning the boards in the downtown area. This doesn't seem weird until the one exception in the bylaw is considered—wheelchairs, if outfitted with skateboards (yes, skateboards) or skateboard wheels, are allowed on downtown streets.

Illegal Idling

In 2010, Toronto city council cut its three-minute idling law down to one minute, which effectively closed loopholes that allowed for weather conditions and idling buses. Residents now have to figure out a better way to defog car windows and warm up the car in the wintertime, and since the fines for flouting this bylaw are substantial, automatic car-starters are not quite the boon they used to be.

Parking Pandemonium

As of October 1, 2010, it became against the law for Toronto residents to park more cars in a driveway than there is garage space, unless residents have a history of parking multiple cars. This is a grandfathered bylaw because it only affects new home construction, but most people who own houses, new or old, have a need, at one time or another, to have multiple vehicles parked in their driveways—the cars of construction workers, real estate agents and prospective buyers are each reasonable exceptions. In fact, this law is so weird that it has Toronto bylaw officers rolling their eyes, and many city council members are having second thoughts and want the law rescinded. The reasons are obvious. Everyone with a driveway can make up an excuse for having a history of parking multiple vehicles in front of their house.

Road Rules
The City of Toronto Act of 2006 is Ontario legislation that classifies roads with a number between one and six according to vehicle-per-day usage and the allowable speed limit. The act dictates the number of times these roads need to be patrolled, and it provides a time limit for repairing potholes, clearing snow and performing other maintenance. Class 1 highways carry traffic of 10,000 or more vehicles per day, and according to the act, must be patrolled three times per week, cleared of snow within three hours and have potholes fixed within four days. Patrols, snow removal and pothole repairs decline in number as the class number goes up. Most residential streets are Class 6 roadways carrying less than 50 vehicles per day, and in this case, the act doesn't apply at all. Readers who reside in Toronto already know this from experience.

Shady Smokes
The Ontario Tobacco Tax Act of 2009 provides courts with the power to suspend the drivers' licences of people found

with illegal cigarettes in their vehicles. According to 2010 Ontario government statistics, almost half of the province's two million tobacco smokers consume illegal cigarettes— and almost all of them are licensed drivers.

Senior Scam

Ontario centenarians (residents over the age of 100) are entitled to a disabled parking permit that's legal anywhere in the province. A good idea in theory, but in 2006, with 4400 permits issued, it was discovered that only 1700 centenarians actually live in Ontario. The province began cross-checking expiry dates (pun intended) and demanding the return of permits by relatives. However, since scams and icebergs show only their tips, a look under the centenarian scam produced a chilly behemoth of titanic proportions. In 2010, there were 535,000 disabled parking permits, now called Accessible Parking Permits, in use, and it's estimated that upward of 50 percent of them are being used illegally. The province has increased the penalties for misuse, but the gaming continues. Shame on those people!

Eco Engines

In 2010, Ontario residents driving electric or plug-in hybrid vehicles began to reap huge benefits by attaching the new "green" licence plates to their cars. The green-on-white plate's benefits include legal access to the high-occupancy vehicle (HOV) lane when there is only one person in the car; the use of recharging facilities at GO Transit stations and at other locations around the province; and designated parking spots at various shopping plazas and some Walmart stores. As of 2010, it also became legal for Ontario residents to convert combustion-engine-powered vehicles to battery-powered vehicles.

Talk and Text

In February 2010, Ontario passed a distracted driving law, and within three months, police services across the province had issued around 15,000 citations, with almost 5000 in Toronto alone. These 15,000 people were caught driving while talking or texting on their cellphones and were charged a fine of at least $155—"at least" because if an officer is feeling particularly cranky, he or she can also charge drivers with careless or dangerous driving. "Driving while distracted" can net transgressors a criminal record as well, so under these circumstances, it's best to keep the cellphone out of sight and out of mind.

Cottage
Life

People are enticed to erect cottages on Georgian Bay Islands by the magnificence at their doorstep, but come spring, some find the magnificence also wants a cottage on a Georgian Bay Island.

THE GREAT OUTDOORS

Goin' Up the Country

The bumper-to-bumper weekend migration from Ontario's southern cities to its northern cottage towns begins in the early spring and continues unabated until Thanksgiving. During the 1950s and 1960s, however, the road heading north was empty, and driving from Toronto to Muskoka or Haliburton was a pleasure as well as an option, because summer vacationers could also take a train anywhere they wanted to go. It's odd how train travel fell out of vogue, with most people choosing instead to spend hours trapped in traffic, but, to some, perhaps even stranger is the provincial government's willingness to embrace road building over the modernization of efficient and environmentally friendly train travel. Money talks, however, and massive road-construction projects that create jobs as well as profit opportunities are the words of the day.

Crapper Law

Any Ontario resident can build one—that essential wilderness device known as a crapper, privy, biffy, backhouse and out-house—but, of course, they have to follow municipal bylaws and the Ontario Building Code when constructing this edifice of relief. An outhouse is considered a Class 1 septic system, and although a building permit isn't needed, the rules of construction are stringent…not that anyone is particularly eager to come looking. All the same, privy-builders are honour-bound to follow the rules of Ontario construction, and even though most residents comply, the ones who use shortcuts should know they're actually creating hazards to the environment because poorly constructed units will leak their waste contaminants into the ground.

Hang that Laundry

Most vacation-area municipalities have for years had bylaws in place that ban people from hanging laundry on outdoor clotheslines. Hanging stuff looks ugly, and it assaults the senses of nature-loving locals, don't cha know? But now, thanks to a 2008 clothesline statute passed by Ontario's Liberal government, it's okay to string up unmen-tionables, swimsuits and wet towels for everyone to see. A provincial statute overrules a municipal bylaw, and though locals might not be happy about it, cottagers and environmentalists sure are.

Watch It Burn

Firefighters who battle blazes in Ontario forests are members of the Ontario Public Service Employees Union (OPSEU), and if that union happens to go on strike (as it did for 54 days in 2002), cottage owners threatened by forest fires have to stand helpless as they watch their cottages go up in smoke. But wait a minute—isn't forest firefighting an essential

service? Apparently not, because even though Smokey the Bear says, "Only you can prevent forest fires," modern cottagers need to take OPSEU and Mother Nature into consideration and put a bit of a different spin on Smokey's meaning. Since most forest fires are started by lightning, Smokey's updated slogan should perhaps read something like this: "Only you can make sure your cottage is well insured and that your policy is up to date and covers all natural disasters." Oh, and under current Ontario law, authorities do not have the power to make people leave their cottages, so even though one might think forced evacuation is the law, guess what, it's not, so if owners want to go up in smoke with their cottages, that's their prerogative.

Name That Town

Gravenhurst is a picturesque town located on the southern shores of Lake Muskoka, but in 1862, it was a nameless village filled with a ragtag collection of trappers' and woods-men's shacks. In that year, and at what is now considered to be the town's first council meeting, a group of residents met in the local tavern to pick a village name because, as they might have said, "You gotta be from someplace, and, hey, word has it they're buildin' a road to here."

At the conclusion of a rowdy discussion over whiskey and beer, the men decided to name their town Gravenhurst, after a fictional name pulled from Washington Irving's novel, *Bracebridge Hall*. The new road that led to Gravenhurst was called the Muskoka Colonization Road, and it eventually connected Toronto with North Bay, spawning villages in the Muskoka area. One of those new towns also used Irving for inspiration, calling itself Bracebridge.

Farther north, the village of Burk's Falls got its name when two original settlers, David Francis Burk and a fellow townsman only known as "Mr. Knight," flipped a coin. There is a lot to love about Burk's Falls because it has everything a cottager could want—clean air and water, magnificent scenery and friendly residents. A good time for all is also mandated in Burk's Falls, and proof of this is found in one of its bylaws that requires all public events to make available light beer and non-alcoholic beverages because such a selection will allow participants to remain at events longer so they can socialize and dance without becoming intoxicated.

A Path Well Travelled

Highways 400 and 11 are Ontario's "holiday highways," and they follow the old Toronto Passage, which was a route that headed north and was used by countless First Nations peoples and fur trappers. Eventually, though, instead of stopping to gnaw on some pemmican, 20th-century travellers began to pull into Webers restaurant, just north of Orillia on Highway 11. Vacationers lined up for this establishment's famous hamburgers, hotdogs and fries, but Webers' popularity turned problematic in the late 1970s when traffic on Highway 11 increased considerably because of Ontario's burgeoning love affair with its cottage country. Stopping at Webers, however, was practically mandatory, and as a result, it was no surprise to face a weekend traffic backup of several kilometres. Webers was a huge headache for what was then called the Ontario Department of Transport (now the Ministry of Transportation), and in 1980, it hatched a plan to stamp out the roadside madness. And so, in June 1981, the simple solution of a box-beam barrier on the median of Highway 11 effectively blocked northbound traffic from crossing the highway into Webers' parking lot. Citizens are always looking for a loophole, though, and soon after the barrier's installation, people driving north began pulling off the road and crossing it on foot, which created even more backup than before.

In 1982, a sturdy chain-link fence was put up, but in a matter of weeks it looked like Swiss cheese for all the holes. No, sir, the public wanted their summer burgers and fries, and any denial of that right was not going to be tolerated. The problem was so bad, however, that rerouting the highway was being considered when fortune suddenly provided a break. Word came down from government sources that the CN Tower had a portion of walkway left over from its construction, and a deal was quickly made for Webers to buy the walkway. In the fall of 1983, and with the blessing of a relieved transportation department, the only privately owned, cross-road walkway in Ontario was installed over Highway 11, and it led into a new parking lot. This helped to ease the highway's traffic problem, and sure, the lineups can still seem torturous, but at Webers, the burgers are charcoal-broiled, and on a hot summer day, this meal of a hamburger and fries is worth the wait.

Bear Wise

Black bears will follow their noses to anywhere that smells like food. They are tempted by the smell of garbage, bird feeders, outdoor barbecues and berry bushes behind cottages. Black bears have no qualms about making themselves right at home if there's good food to be had. Because of this, most municipalities in bear country have bylaws in effect that declare feeding bears an offence, but, unfortunately, people persist in thinking these animals are akin to Winnie the Pooh. Feeding bears is considered dangerous for a reason. If fed repeatedly, bears associate people with food, and lose their wariness of humans while still maintaining their unpredictable and predatory natures. Predator bears are a nightmare for cottagers, and if stalked by one, people should call 911 immediately because the half-starved creature lurking in the woods bears absolutely no resemblance to Pooh.

Funny
Food

*Watermelon—it's a good fruit. You eat, you drink, you
wash your face.*

–Enrico Caruso, opera singer

PONDERING OUR PLATES

Mutated Munchies

"Good things grow in Ontario" is the slogan used by Foodland Ontario, a promotional program pushed by the Ontario Ministry of Agriculture, Food and Rural Affairs. Almost everyone recognizes the catchphrase, and it's usually a comforting reminder that good things do, indeed, grow in the province.

Most people also recognize the old *Frankenstein* movie starring Boris Karloff, but how many are aware that a different incarnation of the monster really exists, not as a manufactured human, but as a genetically modified seed or organism (GMO)? "It's alive! It's alive!" everywhere thanks to chemical companies producing new-age weed killers from glyphosate, a weak organic acid that destroys the ability of plants, particularly perennials, to photosynthesize sunlight. Spray glyphosate on mature crops and say goodbye to weeds. In a perfect world, however, coating emerging crops seems like the better solution. The problem is that doing so would also kill the crops along with the weeds. Scientists have therefore come up with a way for crops to remain resistant to glyphosate by implanting a gene in them that causes healthy plants to be immune to the effects of the weed killer. North American farmers annually use 100 million tonnes of glyphosate on crops such as wheat, corn, soybeans and sugar beets, all of which are ingredients that go into processed foods that Ontarians consume on a daily basis. Many consumers are leery, and with good reason, because little thought or study has been given to the long-term effects of this chemical, and no one wants to become a real-life

Frankenstein's monster. If it's true that you are what you eat, somewhere down the road, Ontarians could be in big trouble. Is this what's meant by "good things grow in Ontario"?

Frankenfoods

GMOs are in approximately 85 percent of the prepared food consumed by Ontarians, and while food scientists call these suspect items "frankenfoods," medical scientists use the term "foods of concern." Does that mean the scientists' fingers are crossed in the hope that nothing is going to happen to the people who consume foods with GMOs in them? Only time will tell.

Cornfused

High-fructose corn syrup derived from GMO corn is the sweetener used in almost every variety of pop, breakfast cereal, bread, ice cream and snack food sold in the province. Medical studies have proved high-fructose corn syrup is making people obese, hardening their arteries and causing allergies, but Ontario's conglomerate food industries keep using it, and this includes its appearance in items that might not be expected, such as baby food.

WEIRD LAWS ABOUT FOOD IN ONTARIO

Eerie Eating

Almost all of Ontario's commercially grown potatoes and corn are implanted with a gene from the DNA of wax moths. This gene causes the crops to manufacture their own insecticide that utilizes the DNA of the soil-dwelling *Bacillus thuringiensis* bacteria. Additionally, most commercially grown tomatoes contain the DNA of various fish and shellfish.

Noxious Nosh

The Toxics Reduction Act of 2010 is legislation that requires particulate matter (solids suspended in a liquid) in foods be listed as toxic, even if that particulate is wheat flour, cocoa, malt or chocolate. Ontario food producers are outraged over this bill and are seeing red, which could soon be the colour of their bottom lines on profit-and-loss statements after trying to sell their "toxic" products to foreign markets.

Plastic Perfection

Certification of organic food is approved by private firms, and the Ontario Ministry of Agriculture, Food and Rural Affairs adheres to federal regulations regarding the production of organically raised food crops. This process works on the farm, but consumers purchasing organic produce at grocery stores should be aware that most stores spray their vegetables with chlorine-laced tap water in order to keep them looking fresh.

Something's Fishy

The Freshwater Fish Marketing Act of 1990 is legislation that established a freshwater-fish marketing board, and the act requires licensed fishermen in Ontario to sell their catch to the board, which is supposed to allow for inspectors to prevent backdoor sales. The act also gives inspectors the power to seize fish they deem as contraband, which can then be held for a period of 90 days. Unfortunately for fishermen, given any trouble, inspectors can lawfully keep seized catches unfrozen, and then return them in an extremely overripe condition.

Reduce, Reuse, Recycle

The Ontario Environmental Protection Act amendment of 1976 was meant to phase out the use of non-refillable beverage containers. It was a good idea that never happened because of political finagling by beverage companies that claimed the act was going to come at the cost of Ontarians' jobs. The act is actually still on the books, and even though businesses can be made to use refillable containers, the government has lacked the will to make it happen, save for beer companies.

The Odd, the Weird
and the Strange

Make crime pay. Become a lawyer.

–Will Rogers, satirist

LOOPY LAWS

The Lowdown

"Loopy" is an English slang word that means "crazy" or "bizarre," and while the Ontario public hopes its government is none of these things, some of the laws that are created in the province often make Ontarians suspect the worst.

Hockey Hooligans

In Toronto, according to bylaw, it's illegal to play hockey on city streets. Offenders can be charged and fined $3.75, the supposed weekly allowance of the average street-hockey-playing kid.

Wacky Workers

Bill 168, an amendment to the Occupational Health and Safety Act, places the responsibility of all workplace violence on the shoulders of Ontario employers. It's an act with good intentions, but workplace violence is not that common, and making an employer liable should something crazy happen, such as an employee's friend, partner or spouse walking into the office and committing an act of violence against them, is just strange.

Lawyers and Losers

The Solicitors Act of 2004 is legislation that legalizes contingency fees as payment to lawyers for trial work that they do. The passing of this law was probably every insurance company's nightmare come true. As the years have gone by, however, Ontarians have seen the floodgates open on personal-injury claims, actions that have actually caused insurance rates to rise considerably. One silver lining found within this snafu is that payouts have been somewhat tempered by Ontario's "loser pays" court practice, meaning that it's customary for judges in the province to award court costs to the winning side. Still, there is a risk in that a

THE ODD, THE WEIRD AND THE STRANGE

plaintiff's lawyer can claim not only the court costs, but also the majority of the monetary reward for services rendered. In other words, the plaintiff would receive practically nothing.

Bulldozed

The University Expropriation Powers Act allows universities and colleges to take over neighbouring properties for expansion purposes—without the consent of the owners. Huh?

Second-hand Sense
In Belleville, residents holding garage sales are required to obtain a permit from city hall and pay a $2 fee. Toronto, on the other hand, doesn't make its citizens obtain a pass to hold a garage sale, but it does limit the number of sales to two per year—any more than that, and residents need a municipal business licence. Both cities' garage-sale bylaws seem like a waste of time, and residents and enforcement officers appear to agree, considering that few charges have ever been recorded.

Vagrant Violations
The Safe Streets Act of 2000 was Toronto's "great crackdown on squeegee kids," but what had previously been a municipal problem soon became a provincial crime. Sure, these people can be irritating, but do they deserve to be arrested, fined and given a criminal record? This law recalls an earlier time when "vagrancy laws" were interpreted by police to mean they could harass anyone for not having proper reason to be in a particular place.

Slapped Silly

Strategic lawsuits against public participation (SLAPPs) are on the rise in Ontario. They are lawsuits aimed at squashing public demonstrations, and are usually launched by property developers. Municipalities, too, have also found SLAPPs handy in silencing reactions to suspect projects. For instance, in 2010, Guelph shut down a plan to turn a forest into an industrial park after resident protestors occupied the territory. Afterward, the city and a private developer selected five participants in that occupation and sued them for $5 million. Legal intimidation is a nasty business, but when used by public servants to scare off legitimate protestors, is it not a crime against democracy? Québec has already passed anti-SLAPP legislation, and Ontario has launched a tribunal to hash out its own version, but the five defendants who were named in the Guelph lawsuit are still shouldering the financial costs of the law.

FUNNY LAWS
The Law of the Land

Some Ontario laws are loopy, whereas others are downright humorous. Ontario and its 444 municipalities usually create bylaws from templates, while the province works with approximately 500,000 old laws. Municipalities use a list of permitted laws. Let's take a look at what the results are.

Communication Breakdown

The Guarantee Act of 1849 was passed by the Legislative Assembly of Upper Canada to facilitate railway construction by guaranteeing bond issues. This set off a rail-laying craze, especially in Ontario, where two companies, Great Western Railway and Grand Trunk Railway, ran parallel tracks that connected the Niagara area and Toronto with the U.S. border in Sarnia. The driving thought behind the Guarantee Act was to incite an increase in trade with the U.S., and this was great, except that the Canadians didn't consider that the Americans might have used a different track width...which, of course, they did. Oops.

Snowball Sins

In 1860, Toronto citizens got a glimpse of the "minder" attitudes of their new Board of Commissioners of Police when it passed Bylaw 322, which outlawed throwing snowballs in city parks.

Shirts vs. Skins

In 1908, the Sons of Freedom, a splinter group of the religious zealots called the Doukhobors, staged a march from Yorkton, Saskatchewan, to Fort William, Ontario, to protest the Canadian government's insistence that they register their property. Upon their arrival at Fort William, 19 of the marchers did what came naturally to Doukhobors, and stripped off their clothing. Those 19 protesters were arrested by police and were found guilty in an Ontario court of indecent exposure. They were sentenced to six months in prison, and even though that should have been the end of the conflict, the Doukhobors had such a reputation for being off-the-scale weird that no Ontario prison would accept them as inmates. Ontario law was stymied. Seeing no way out of the situation, Fort William authorities had the police round up the entire group, along with the 19 unwanted prisoners, and everyone was shipped back to Yorkton on a nice, warm train.

Man the Fort

Ajax is a lovely lakeside town near Toronto, and in order to keep it sitting pretty, the city council has enacted a bylaw that declares it illegal to fortify property, rig explosive traps or plant land mines. It's a little weird, but these days, perhaps people can't be too careful? Erring on the side of caution, many other Ontario municipalities are following Ajax's suit, and are also passing anti-fortification bylaws. Some people sure have a lot of time on their hands.

Wading through the Weeds
In Amherstburg, it's against the law to allow lawn weeds to grow higher than 20 centimetres. This is an odd law because if weeds of that size are present, it likely means the house is derelict, haunted or the scene of a grow-op, and either no one lives in the house to trim the weeds, or no one cares about them in the first place.

Bready Blunder
The city of Whitby declares it illegal to throw bread to ducks and geese, and this law has people quacking in front of a judge and lighter in the wallet for ignoring what the town council calls the Waterfowl Bylaw. Residents, however, prefer to call it the Waterfoul Bylaw.

Musical Mayhem

Hamilton's bylaw enforcement officers so broadly interpret this city's anti-noise legislation that people practicing on violins and pianos have been subject to fines and desist orders. It might be considered wise for residents considering a go at the bagpipes to practice them outside city limits.

Silence is Golden

Belleville's consolidated-noise bylaw is a municipal act that requires complete silence—no bells, whistles, horns, squealing tires, barking dogs or lawn mowers—within 30 metres of a dwelling. The exceptions are the calls of newsboys, street hawkers, folks Christmas carolling and church bells on Sundays. The law even provides for the issuing of a ticket if an officer is disturbed by the noise while conducting his or her investigation. A twofer fine!

Fencing Felony

Figure this one out: a Toronto bylaw reads that a front-yard fence cannot be more than 1.2 metres high, but the first 2.4 metres cannot be higher than 99 centimetres if the material is opaque. Toronto council members should stop smoking Amherstburg's 20-centimetre-high weeds.

Border Dispute

All municipalities in the province, according to the Ontario Line Fences Act, are required to have official "fence viewers" on call to arbitrate fencing disagreements between neighbours. Communities can choose to opt out by passing a bylaw that states neighbours are to halve their fencing costs, but many, including Toronto, employ fence viewers (whose costs are to be met by the disputing neighbours) on a per diem basis. Fence viewers, who always work in teams of three, can help neighbours decide on the type, height, cost and length of fences, as well as who owns whatever straddles a fence line, such as trees or shrubs. Property boundaries, however, are not the business of a fence viewer. The final decisions of fence viewers are binding under law, but can be appealed. Want to be a fence viewer when you grow up?

Struck by Lightning

In 1990, Ontario's Lightning Rods Act was created, and it requires that the Ontario Fire Marshal license lightning-rod installers and inspect their installations. It also states that lightning-rod buyers must be supplied with a 10-year, money-back guarantee should the rods fail. "Gee, Mary, everything burned but those cheap lightning rods. What luck, now we can get our money back."

Puddle Prohibition

No puddles allowed in Markham. A case of the mosquito-vectored West Nile virus was diagnosed there in 2008, and now, short of bylaw officers to enforce the "no puddles" law, the town has empowered its cadre of parking enforcement officers to act as the puddle police. This means they can now wield their power on illegally parked cars, as well as poke around backyards while look-ing for puddle-pushers.

Shut Up

The town of Caledon, a rural masterpiece northwest of Toronto, insists that residents and visitors maintain proper decorum through a nuisance bylaw that bans crying, yelling, hooting, shouting or loud speaking in, or adjacent to, any pub-lic street or place, or in, or on, any private place. Is it crying out or actual tears that are banned? Can it be that happiness is the law in Caledon? The town's picture-perfect ambience would have you believe so. Be happy in Caledon, it's the law.

Weird
Court

*Only lawyers and mental defectives are automatically
exempt for jury duty.*

–George Bernard Shaw, playwright

TRIALS AND TRIBULATIONS

The Law of the Land

Each Canadian province has three levels of court: provincial, which hears most criminal cases and deals with family law and financial matters; superior, which manages the more serious criminal and civil cases, as well as divorce; and appeals, which, of course, hears the appeals from the two lower courts. For the most part, all three are well-oiled machines, but, much to the chagrin of the public, each is guilty of occasionally soaking up both sensibility and tax dollars.

Turf War

Ontario's Rivers and Streams Act of 1884 was provincial legislation that ended up becoming the law that allowed public access to the waterways of Canada. How an Ontario law became the law of Canada is an interesting story. It began, as many stories do, with an exchange of action between two main characters—in this case, two Scotsmen named Boyd Caldwell and Peter McLaren.

Both men were loggers and owned timber rights on the Mississippi River (the body of water that flows into the Ottawa River, not the one that winds its way into the Gulf of Mexico). Anyway, the instigator in this tale was Caldwell, who reacted to McLaren's barring of other loggers from using his section of the river. McLaren had made improvements—log chutes, dams, diversions and booms—and was not amenable toward allowing other loggers to capitalize on his upgrades. McLaren effectively blocked the river, and he did it with the help of legal ammunition, courtesy of an injunction from the Court of Chancery, a federal judicial body that dealt with land transfers, mortgages, civil disputes and estate issues.

Stymied, Caldwell appealed to Ontario premier Oliver Mowat, who convinced his provincial legislature to pass the Rivers and Streams Act of 1881, giving loggers the right to use waterways, subject to a toll paid to the owner of any river improvements. McLaren was outraged, and his appeal to the Supreme Court of Canada and the government of John A. Macdonald resulted in the Ontario Rivers and Streams Act being disallowed in order to protect the sanctity of private property. Now everyone except McLaren was outraged. Mowat and Macdonald began slinging mud over federal and provincial toe-stepping, the Ontario legislature was threatening to withhold tax money, loggers were fighting on the Mississippi and newspaper editorials were suggesting that Macdonald go jump in a lake. Meanwhile, however, Caldwell quietly appealed to the Queen's Privy Council in London, England, and after a lengthy discussion, it declared Ontario's Rivers and Streams Act to be lawful. Caldwell had gone over the heads of local politicians and jurists, and had garnered a legal decision that ended up affecting every waterway in Canada.

In 1884, a delighted Mowat reintroduced the Ontario River and Streams Act, and a grumpy Macdonald threw in the towel. Caldwell started pushing logs again, McLaren sold out and Canadians freely learned to swim and fly-fish.

Better Late Than Never?
In 1975, Enbridge Gas Distribution Inc., with the blessing of the Ontario Energy Board, routinely started to charge customers a five percent late-payment fee. One day late, and five percent of the bill was added to the next month's statement. This resulted in annual amounts that exceeded Ontario's Criminal Code usury cap of 60 percent. (Usury is an excessive interest rate, and it's actionable under Ontario law but was completely ignored by Enbridge for almost 20 years.) In 1994, however, a class-action lawsuit was launched by concerned citizens who wanted to bring the giant gas company to task.

The Supreme Court found Enbridge guilty of usury in 1998, but the case was referred to a lower court for fine determination. However, the judge of that court agreed with the Enbridge defence that the company had only been following the orders of its regulator, the Ontario Energy Board, and the case was dismissed. A second suit was launched, and in 2004, it again reached the Supreme Court, which did not support Enbridge's claim that they had been following orders (or what the court called the "Eichmann defence"). The case was turned over to a lower court, and Enbridge was levied a penalty of $100 million, the amount of profit made by the company through its usury practices since 1994, the year the first suit was launched, which was when Enbridge should have been spurred into some other action than continuing its late-fee charge. The court didn't call Enbridge dumb as wood, but the amount of the fine is enough to supply the insinuation.

They Never Learn

You would think Enbridge's case would be a lesson learned for other companies, but apparently not. In 1981, Ontario's 80 municipal electrical distribution companies began to routinely charge customers six to seven percent per month in late payments—and they continued to do so even after the Enbridge case was closed. Not surprisingly, concerned citizens launched a class-action lawsuit, in 2008. Ontario's Supreme Court found the distributors guilty of usury in 2010, and levied them a $17 million fine, $5 million of which was to go toward legal fees, and the remainder of which was to go into a United Way program to assist low-income families in paying their hydro bills. Toronto Hydro, which had the deepest pockets, was required to ante up $7.75 million of the $17 million but has since applied to the hydro regulator, the Ontario Energy Board, for permission to pass that payment on to customers. That's some nerve.

The Cornwall Incident

In 1993, Constable Perry Dunlop, a Cornwall policeman, overheard two fellow officers talking about a sexual abuse case that was never investigated and that involved a local priest. After a little digging, Dunlop determined that charges had not gone forward because hush money was paid by the church diocese to the victim. Dunlop made some inquiries, and he found out that the accused child-molester priest was still on the job and in daily contact with children. A father of three, it was natural for Dunlop to be concerned about the continuation of any abuse, so he asked his chief why the case's files had not been turned over to the Children's Aid Society, as per provincial rules.

The chief told Dunlop, in as many words, to mind his own business and forget about the case. He couldn't forget, however, and his conscience drove him to turn the files over to the Children's Aid Society. In doing so, Dunlop was pilloried by the police, sued and slandered, abandoned by his municipal government, locked up for seven months and the victim of threats against his family and health—all because he blew the whistle on a cover-up that eventually exposed a cabal of pedophiles who were part of the highest strata of Cornwall society.

On April 14, 2005, Parliament ordered an inquiry into the Cornwall affair. Called Project Truth, the investigation lasted five years, revealed 50 victims and more than 24 perpetrators, filed 71 charges and spent approximately $53 million in tax dollars on legal fees for victims, defendants, judges and the Cornwall police. As for Dunlop, the constable who turned over the dirty rock, he has so far been the only one to ever see the inside of a jail cell.

The Million-dollar Fly in the Bottle

In 2004, a Windsor hairstylist spotted a fly in an unopened 19-litre water jug that was supplied by the Culligan water company. Although he had consumed this brand of water for some 15 years, the hairstylist was so revolted by this one jug that he became susceptible to bouts of depression and ended up suing Culligan. It was the beginning of an outrageous case that ultimately cost Ontario taxpayers more than $1 million in court time and public defender fees.

The first court to hear the case sympathized with the hairstylist and awarded $300,000 in damages. The case then went before the Ontario Court of Appeal, which dismissed the claim. Not satisfied, the hairstylist took his case to Ottawa and to the Supreme Court, where, in 2008, a full panel of nine judges once again dismissed the case. In the end, the debacle resulted in four years of wasted court time and tax dollars, all because of a fly that was observed but never consumed.

The Cumberland Case

Michel Giroux and Manon Bourdeau met at the Carlsbad Springs Hotel near Ottawa, where Bourdeau worked as a bartender and Giroux sold drugs. The pair hit it off, moved into a small house in Cumberland, about 10 kilometres from the hotel, and lived the high life until Bourdeau became pregnant. Unprepared for fatherhood, Giroux went on a crack-cocaine bender that only served to get him deep in debt to his drug supplier. Deciding he was going to snitch on his supplier, Giroux lost the opportunity to do so when a person or persons unknown caught him off guard at his house on January 16, 1990, and killed him execution-style with two blasts from a sawed-off shotgun. Bourdeau, seven months pregnant, was shot dead while asleep, and her mangled body, along with Giroux's, laid in the house for two days until the pair was found by a neighbour. Forensics combed the house for clues, but found nothing except the blurred imprint of a size 9 or 10 Nike sneaker. It was a whodunit that most people probably thought had been committed by the drug supplier. Police assumed this as well, especially after one of Giroux's associates at the Carlsbad Springs Hotel confessed to driving the drug supplier and his enforcers to Giroux's house on the night of the murders. It was a confession that prosecutors used in court, even after the driver later admitted to engineering a rip-off of the drug dealer in order to finance a getaway to Vancouver.

Four people faced charges in the case—the alleged drug dealer, Robert Stewart, his alleged enforcer, Richard Mallory, and another alleged dealer-enforcer team, Richard Trudel and James Sauve, who were involved because Trudel's brother had pointed fingers at them (accusations the brother later recanted because he admitted to being miffed with Trudel, and wanted to punish him). At this point, the police had nothing but circumstantial evidence that was based on accusations by unreliable people. A connection between Stewart and Mallory and Trudel and Sauve couldn't even be made, so prosecutors launched separate trials, starting with Trudel and Sauve in a case that dragged on for 15 months through 1997 and 1998. This trial produced 100 volumes of worthless evidence, 70 unreliable witnesses, 194 exhibits of a dubious nature and 50,000 pages of Crown documents. Defence lawyers, at times, became so incensed with prosecutors the two sides almost came to blows. The jury took 12 days to decide the fate of Trudel and Sauve, and both received life sentences. Afterward, the presiding judge was so relieved that he threw an "end to tediousness" party to celebrate the closing of the case. The taxpayers, however, were out millions of dollars, and the financial drain continued when the two were granted new trials because of mistakes made by the presiding judge. In 2004, prosecutors went after Stewart and Mallory in a trial that lasted three years. This trial saw 299 suspect exhibits, 66 undependable witnesses and 31 days on the witness stand by the most undependable person of all, the alleged driver of the getaway car who had been called back from a witness protection program and who had already cost taxpayers over $400,000. Things got so nasty, the defence and the prosecution both filed misconduct charges with the Law Society of Upper Canada, which cost taxpayers even more millions. The end result was that Stewart and Mallory also received life sentences, but their lawyers filed immediate appeals.

In 2007, an Ottawa judge stayed the 16-year prosecution of Trudel and Sauve, citing the ravages of time and improprieties by the justice system. Trudel and Sauve were released from prison, and Stewart and Mallory gained their freedom soon afterward. The pairs' trials cost them 16 years of their lives, Ontario taxpayers paid more than $30 million in the case, and yet the financial drain goes on into the second decade of the 21st century. Both Trudel and Sauve have filed $32-million "unlawful prosecution" suits against the province, with the same expected to come from Stewart and Mallory. The most expensive trials in Ontario history seem endless, and this one could see Ontario taxpayers on the hook for $70 million—if they're lucky.

WEIRD ONTARIO LEGAL EVENTS

Political Pugilists

During the 19th century, the most common criminal charge in Ontario was common assault. Everyone liked to fight, especially in taverns. In the mid-1800s, taverns could be found in every village and town, and on every eight-kilometre stretch of coach road. With no movies, TV or radio, taverns were places of entertainment. Drink a few pints, nibble on some lunch at the bar and watch a good fight—what more could a patron want? Fights were often about the politics of the time, and Ontario's distinguished gentlemen and politicos weren't exempt from boiling blood. Take a look in the court records of 19th-century magistrates and you'll find the names of many of the province's luminaries. Ontario politics were born and raised in taverns, and in the 19th century, they were the sites of many unofficial courts of law.

Crackdown on Crystal Balls

Near the end of the 19th century, a rumour began to circulate through northern Ontario general stores that gypsies were stealing children. Gypsies, or people claiming to be gypsies, sometimes visited northern towns as part of travelling entertainment troupes, and there was a general air of mistrust directed at them by villagers. In order to calm anxious mothers who were demanding the protection of their children, many town officials passed fortune-telling and palm-reading bylaws that prohibited, except by permit, both of these activities for payment. The thought process was that even though a gypsy could obtain a short-term licence, it didn't take long to expire, which would then leave him or her unable to make a living, and he or she would move on, meaning that local children were safe once more. Today, fortune tellers are ubiquitous in Ontario; their neon signs light up windows in almost every town. A few of those original anti-gypsy villages have even become cities, such as Sudbury and Kenora, and while their old bylaws are no longer active, they are still on the books.

Home for the Holidays

During the early 20th century, "half holidays" were de rigueur in Ontario, and municipalities passed bylaws that forced all businesses to close for the afternoon on a particular day. On that day, bustling towns were suddenly empty of people at noon, and the atmosphere was that of a ghost town. The city of Trenton later one-upped everywhere else by declaring Mondays "whole-day holidays." In 1960, however, Trenton reworked that bylaw, and today, only grocery stores enjoy Mondays off.

Top-down Town

On a hot, cicada-buzzing afternoon in July 1991, University of Guelph student Gwen Jacobs had a notion to go for a cooling stroll, sans T-shirt. Bare-breasted, she walked across the campus, down the hill and into town. While attracting a following, Jacobs got most of the way through town before a woman wheeling a baby stroller complained to a police officer. The cop charged Jacobs with indecent exposure, and if convicted, she could have faced a stiff fine, a possible jail sentence and a criminal record. The court did, indeed, find Jacobs guilty, but it delayed sentencing to allow for appeal. In 1996, the Supreme Court of Ontario overturned her conviction, granting women the same right as men to bare their chests. Three cheers for Gwen Jacobs! Why hasn't the University of Guelph yet installed a bronze plaque to honour her historical walk? Coventry, England, has one in place to honour Lady Godiva's ride, and historians doubt she actually existed!

Refrigerator Regulations

Tragedies involving children often inspire municipalities to create bylaws that are usually parroted, post-haste, by other communities. None, however, was more quickly adopted than Windsor's hinge-removal bylaw. In 1953, two children were playing with an abandoned refrigerator when they climbed inside and the door closed on them. Unable to open it from the inside, the trapped children died. Within days of the tragedy, every municipality in Ontario had passed a bylaw that required the removal of hinges from unused refrigerators. It's unfortunate that tragedy often needs to strike before what seems like an obvious bylaw is passed.

A Meaty Matter

In 2001, the Food Safety and Quality Act was passed, and what it meant for Ontarians was that butchering animals for home consumption was allowed, but sharing the bounty was illegal. Fast-forward to 2009, when Carlsbad Springs resident Major Mark Tijssen threw in with a friend to buy a hog to butcher. Tijssen had grown up on a farm, so he knew what to do, but problems arose when his neighbour, a man who thought pork should come frozen in boxes from the store, complained to the police. The police passed the complaint on to the Ministry of Natural Resources (MNR), and it dispatched investigators so quickly that they caught Tijssen's butchering partner leaving Tijssen's property with 18 kilograms of meat. Two days later, MNR officials, accompanied by police, raided Tijssen's property and charged him with failure to have an animal inspected before butchering, running an unlicensed slaughterhouse and illegally distributing meat. In 2011, Tijssen is still fighting the charges against something that for hundreds of years was considered a basic act necessary for survival.

Bumbling Braggart

In Vaughan, in 2010, a 19-year-old man bragged on a BMW online chat website that he drove his own BMW at 100 kilometres per hour over the posted speed limit. He was reported to Vaughan police by a U.S. website user. Police reviewed the teenager's online message, considered it tantamount to a confession and promptly charged him with careless driving. The young man pleaded guilty, lost his driver's licence for six months and received a $1000 fine.

Triple Threat

In a 2010 case known only as *AA v. BB*, the Supreme Court of Ontario decided that a child can have three parents. AA had donated an egg to BB and wanted visitation rights to the matured egg, once it became a child. The donor won visitation rights, and the egg was eventually the recipient of an extra parent.

Secret Society

At Queen's Park in Toronto, in 2010, prior to the infamous G20 summit, Premier Dalton McGuinty reworked the Public Works Protection Act and pushed through secret legislation that gave police unusual powers of arrest if protesters came within five metres of a protective fence. So hush-hush was this law that many police officers were never informed of its parameters and went about the summit demonstrations corralling and arresting innocent bystanders as if no restrictions for such actions had ever been put into place. As a result, dozens of lawsuits were launched against the police, and—surprise, surprise—will most likely end up costing taxpayers millions to settle.

Door-knocker Denial

In Beaconsfield, a picturesque farming community north of Tillsonburg, residents in the mid-1960s got so fed up with door-to-door peddlers and crews distributing flyers that they demanded an end to the problem. Municipal officials complied, and a bylaw was promptly passed that banned door-to-door visitations by salespeople who lacked a special permit. Permits, however, are only available for representatives of non-profit organizations, so those commercial door-bangers are but a memory in the town.

Crafty Contracting

In 1996, Wanda Liczyk, a North York municipal financial officer, met Michael Saunders, a salesman from the U.S., and the pair began an affair of the heart that precipitated a Toronto city-hall patronage scandal of epic proportions.

Love is fine, but not when one of the people involved is responsible for spending tax dollars, as Liczyk was, on what their paramour is selling, which, in the case of Saunders, was computer services. Liczyk kept him well supplied with North York city hall computer-service contracts, and in 1998, when North York became part of Metropolitan Toronto, Liczyk moved into the big time as treasurer of the City of Toronto. Without engaging in a bidding process, she promptly awarded Saunders and his partner a $3.8-million contract for a computer tax-collection system. The city also signed a contract with Ball Hue and Associates to keep the system up and running, and the entire deal, thanks to fine print in the contract, ballooned into a $10-million debacle.

In the meantime, Liczyk had become chummy with Dash Domi (the brother of hockey great Tie Domi), who was a salesman for MFP Financial Services Ltd. of Mississauga. Toronto civic employees needed new computers, and Domi was on the spot to provide financing for a $43-million deal. His contract also came complete with a fine-print maintenance clause that increased spending to $85 million over five years. By this time, Liczyk had the tongues of city councillors wagging, and they were demanding an inquiry. In September 2002, the inquiry was launched and went on for two years, costing Toronto taxpayers $20 million. The reason it took so long was because all the witnesses disappeared. Hue, from Ball Hue and Associates, fled to China, and Saunders went back to the U.S., from where he refused to budge. The inquiry eventually found Liczyk guilty of inattentiveness, and criminal charges were recommended, but a four-year investigation by the Ontario Provincial Police—that cost Ontario taxpayers even more millions—went nowhere. In the end, on April 25, 2010, the Institute of Chartered Accountants of Ontario fined Liczyk $22,000 and suspended her accountant's licence for six months. The original inquiry had also pointed fingers at some Toronto city council members, but nothing came of those accusations. One hopes that since then, the public's focus on the ethics problems within Toronto's city hall has caused councillors to smarten up and adopt stringent rules of conduct—it's just too bad that wising up had to cost Toronto taxpayers over $100 million.

A-Hunting
We Will Go

When I was 12, I went hunting with my father and we shot a bird. He was laying there and something struck me. Why do we call this fun to kill this creature who was as happy as I was when I woke this morning?

—Marv Levy, pro football coach

THE FOREST FORMULA

Not so Fast

So you want to hunt in Ontario? Do you have fond memories of being in the bush with your dad, potting your first rabbit, and now you want to recreate those same memories for your child or grandchild? The old shotgun is still in the closet, so why not grab the kid, load up the car and hit the trail? But wait just a second. Firstly, that shotgun that's been in the closet all these years is going to get you into deep doo-doo should it see daylight. Ontario requires gun owners to have a federal possession and acquisition licence (PAL) if they want to take their guns outside or if they want to buy a new one. To obtain a PAL, hunters have to take the Canadian Firearms Safety Course, a one-day, all-encompassing workshop that takes its students through proper gun care, execution, maintenance and storage. Once the safety course is completed, PAL applicants fill out the required forms, include a picture and a reference in the package, mail everything out and then wait. Sooner—or sometimes later—the permit arrives, and hunters are in business. Or are they?

To hunt in Ontario, outdoor enthusiasts also need to pass the 20-hour Ontario Hunter Education Course and secure an "outdoor card" that's available at ServiceOntario kiosks or sporting goods stores. The option also exists to take a "twofer" course from an instructor who is licensed to teach both the Canadian Firearms Safety Course and the Ontario Hunter Education Course. To find an instructor, hunters should contact ServiceOntario over the phone or online. About 300 instructors are located across the province.

Licence Litany

To fish in Ontario, residents are required to obtain an outdoor card, as well as a fishing licence. The only exceptions to this rule are if the fisher is under 18 or over 65.

Read the List

The Ontario Species at Risk Act of 2007 is legislation that provides for the protection of the province's endangered wildlife. The list of animals is long and disheartening but worth a review by hunters and fishers because penalties for violating it can be harsh, even if an endangered animal is killed by mistake. In other words, turtles with antennas should not be disturbed because the Ontario government has instituted a wireless tracking system for "at risk" amphibians.

You Can't Miss Him

Sightings of the elusive, large-footed hairy beast called Sasquatch in western Canada and Bigfoot in Ontario are on the rise, and hunters might be a little trigger-happy in their attempts to bag the creature. Ontario has a law against shooting at the colour red, but nothing exists to prevent hunters from shooting at Bigfoot, so if you have long hair and a large stature and you like to grunt in the backcountry, you're well advised during the fall hunting season to wear a red vest to avoid being confused with Bigfoot and getting shot at.

Weekend Wilderness

In 2010, the Ontario Ministry of Natural Resources relaxed its ban on Sunday hunting to allow municipalities to permit or prohibit Sunday hunting at their own discretion. Many communities jumped at the chance, and it's now a rare Sunday that Bambi gets to rest.

Gun Control

In Elliot Lake, the misuse of firearms is taken seriously. So seriously, in fact, that the town passed a bylaw outlawing the discharge of any type of gun within Elliot Lake limits. To be well on the side of safety, the town council also added into the bylaw every other weapon they could think of, including a kids' bow and arrow set. Should the Elliot Lake bylaw enforcement cops catch any children shooting arrows in the backyard, mom and dad can expect a fine of up to $5000. Here's hoping a prime specimen of buck doesn't wander through the yard!

Weird
Water

*I never drink water because of the disgusting things that
fish do in it.*

–W.C. Fields, comedian

GETTING YOUR FEET WET

Suspicious Septics

The distribution of human waste via septic systems is the law in Ontario, and there are no exceptions allowed. A flushed toilet empties into a tank, bacteria breaks down the solids and the liquid overflows into leaching beds that soak into wide areas of land. This process wasn't so bad when rural areas were sparsely populated, but that has changed, and many of these communities are much more densely inhabited, with one in four the site of a leaching bed. The same one in four residents of these rural areas depend on wells for their drinking water, and a good portion of these wells are now polluted, with many more hovering on the brink of acceptable nitrogen and pathogen contents. Twenty-five percent of Ontario's population is in desperate straits over its drinking water, and, distressingly, the government has agreed to an amendment to the Water Resources Act that shifts the responsibility for clean water onto well owners. So although it's unlawful to allow pollutants to seep into well water, in the same breath, it's illegal to not use a septic system, one of the main causes of contaminated well water. Allowing the installation of anaerobic systems that don't pollute groundwater would be a welcome amendment to the Ontario Building Code and would probably be celebrated across the province.

Throne Time

In the spring of 1996, hundreds of Collingwood residents hit the bathrooms when a parasite called *Cryptosporidium parvum* infiltrated the town's water supply. Although not usually fatal, *C. parvum* can put its victims on the throne for days—it's essentially *la turista*, sans Mexico.

A few weeks after the Collingwood outbreak, residents in Sioux Lookout and a few other small towns in northern areas of Ontario found parasites in their drinking water, and the provincial government spent millions of tax dollars putting them back on track. In 2000, Ontario's Ministry of the Environment warned the Mike Harris government of potentially greater drinking-water problems, but it was a warning the government ignored and sorely regretted.

The Walkerton Fiasco

Most residents of Walkerton have always considered their water some of the best on the planet. The town, nestled on the banks of the Saugeen River, a river that some regarded as being so clean that its water was drinkable, exuded healthy living, and Walkerton was feeling no pain. But then, in May 2000, people began to get violently ill. The culprits turned out to be *Escherichia coli*, or *E. coli*, and *Campylobacter jejuni*, both virulent forms of bacteria that live in the guts of animals. Walkerton is a farming community with lot of cows and, consequently, plenty of *E. coli*. Unfortunately for residents, the two brothers who worked part-time at the Walkerton Public Utilities Commission, and who were responsible for treatment of the community's drinking water, weren't doing their jobs. The brothers were in charge of maintaining the pump, the supply of chlorine and the chlorine-metering system, a device they were negligent in monitoring. Their sloppiness allowed bacteria to enter Walkerton's drinking water, and the mistake ended up killing seven, sickening 2300, devastating the town and costing Ontario taxpayers almost $65 million. What later came to light was that the brothers knew about the bacteria contamination a few days before the outbreak but failed to warn consumers.

The good thing that came out of the Walkerton tragedy was Ontario's Safe Drinking Water Act of 2002, but it's definitely weird that no previous legislation existed that ensured Ontario residents were drinking safe water. The Drinking Water Surveillance Program that was instituted in 1996 and run by the Ministry of the Environment routinely screened municipal drinking water across the province, but Mike Harris' Conservatives decreased this ministry's budget by half as part of a cost-cutting program, and within a year, water testing had been severely downsized. In 1997, the Harris government scrapped the Drinking Water Surveillance Program completely and passed the responsibility for clean drinking water over to municipal governments. What this meant for smaller communities was that part-time workers were in charge of the water. Remember the brothers at the centre of the Walkerton scandal? And although the Drinking Water program was no more, it's known that Ministry of the Environment inspectors actually tested Walkerton's water in 1998, and traces of *E. coli* bacteria were found even then. The inspectors left recommendations about what needed to be done but failed to follow up on fixes that were never made.

Bubbly Pink in Stratford
On a March morning in 2005, bubbly pink water poured from the taps of Stratford residents, and the municipal works department suddenly went into overdrive. City workers were ordered to open fire hydrants, the chief medical officer went on TV to warn residents not to drink the water and firemen, postal workers and volunteers went door to door with water advisories. Stratford schools were closed, the hospital outsourced its treatment for various ailments and depots were set up to distribute bottled water. The culprits in this town oddity turned out to be a car wash with an illegal high-pressure pump and a negligent employee who forgot to turn off a soap valve. The fouling of drinking water is a crime

as declared by Ontario's newer, Walkerton-inspired Clean Water Act, and for causing the tap water to be bubbly and pink, the car wash received a hefty fine of $75,000.

Since then, the Clean Water Act has been revamped, and in 2006, its legislation divided Ontario into 40 sections, which were mostly based on conservation areas. It also provided a way to determine threats to water quality by way of an assessment report. The report uses a table of circumstances to predict threats to drinking-water sources, and this crystal-ball approach is intended to head off another Walkerton fiasco, should an outbreak seem likely. There are built-in parameters, however, and the assessment report fails to factor in petrochemical or nuclear-power threats. Predictions are also confined to land-based problems such as farming, gravel pits and goose poop. Additionally, the entire Great Lakes system, from which many Ontario municipalities get their water, is exempt from threat evaluation. Industries that use Great Lakes water are also exempt.

Environmental Time Bomb

In 1868, the Ontario Mining Act came into effect, and it allowed the prospecting, blasting and clear-cutting of trees on Crown land. The act, however, didn't provide for the remediation of abandoned mines, of which Ontario now has thousands. The freshwater capital of the world, Ontario is a valuable asset, but its water is threatened because of these deserted mines.

When a mine is in use, water is pumped from it, but when it's left idle for a long period of time, groundwater leaches out mineral dusts and nasty chemicals that slowly migrate into rivers and lakes. Combine those pollutants with the almost 2500 landfill sites and the roughly 1000 buried or abandoned historic landfills the province has lost track of, and the threats being presented to Ontario's water increase considerably. Add in the thousands of kilometres of old logging and mining roads that are eroding into streams and rivers, and the risks being presented to Ontario's environment seem close to insurmountable. If not for the goading of environmental groups such as the Lake Ontario Waterkeepers, residents of the province might still be in the dark about the reality of the hazards to their water quality.

Radical Radioactivity

There is a pipe in Port Hope that spews radioactive leach water into Lake Ontario. The now-defunct Port Hope–based Eldorado Mining and Refining Ltd. company processed the uranium used to make the Hiroshima and Nagasaki atom bombs, and it buried the hot residuals underground. The gushing pipe, once buried, drains water from that site, and although the pipe used to run several kilometres into Lake Ontario, winter ice has exposed and broken it, so now it's on the beach for all to see. Why doesn't anyone in power seem to care about a radioactive substance being dumped into a lake that millions of people depend on for drinking water?

The Eldorado Mining and Refining Ltd. plant, whose name was later changed to Eldorado Nuclear Limited, refined its nuclear materials from 1933 to 1988, and in addition to the mine's water problems, and in spite of dire warnings from industry experts, Atomic Energy of Canada Limited is endeavouring to remediate Port Hope with a dig-and-move program that costs $260 million—even though it has been cautioned that the project will likely expose the town's residents to radiation.

Bad Brown

Brownfields, abandoned factory sites that are found in almost every Ontario town and city, are the relics of bustling industries. These lots now sit forlorn, bare of vegetation and ready to cause trouble if disturbed. Brownfields include anything from war munitions factories that manufactured batteries, poisonous gasses, radium-painted dials and explosives made from toluene, to recycling depots that harbour heavy and deadly metals from a more careless era. Long ignored but slowly causing environmental damage, brownfields are forcing municipalities to deal with them through soil remediation, an expensive procedure that has so far cost Ontario taxpayers millions of dollars.

One Day in Cambridge

Rapid community growth usually puts a strain on water-treatment and delivery systems, so many towns and cities in Ontario have taken a page from the popular European odd-and-even vehicle-driving days and adapted the law for the watering of lawns and gardens, the filling of swimming pools and the washing of cars. What this means is that residents with odd-numbered street addresses can use their outside water on odd-numbered calendar days, and vice versa for even-numbered addresses and days. The city of Cambridge, a 1973 amalgamation of the towns of Galt, Preston, Hespeler and Blair, has grown so fast, though, that it outpaced this system. The remedy is a bylaw that's in effect from the end of May to the end of September that states all of the aforementioned "water-related" activities can be performed just once per week, in the mornings and evenings, and only on days determined by the last digit in a resident's street address.

WEIRD LAWS ABOUT WATER

Words of Wisdom

The Ontario Water Resources Commission, originally headed by London, Ontario, resident and premier, John Robarts, owes its 1953 formation to words of advice given by former U.S. president Dwight Eisenhower to former Ontario premier Leslie Frost at an Ottawa dinner party: "Don't let them ruin your water, Leslie. We have ruined ours in the States."

Oily Observations

The Ontario Oil, Gas and Salt Resources Act of 1997 is legislation that states the rules and regulations for the drilling of gas and oil. To insure against accidents, drillers are required to ante up a trust fund to cover the cost of unexpected repairs or remediation. The required amount of the fund when the project involves drilling into water is $200,000, which seems like a paltry sum, considering the public knows it cost British Petroleum (BP) billions to clean up its 2010 oil spill in the Gulf of Mexico.

Pollution Problems

The town of Port Colborne, on Lake Erie, draws its drinking water from the Welland Canal, disinfects it with chlorine and distributes it through a century-old water main. During those times when the Welland Canal suffers from ship pollution, such as oil or chemical spills, the town gets its water from an emergency reservoir and discourages lawn watering, clothes washing and bathing. Port Colborne also prohibits the sharing of water, so even when a crisis hits, it's only one person to a tub or else that individual could face a $200 fine. The bylaw also allows residents to be charged a $350 fine for throwing "noisome" (noxious) objects into the water supply.

Sprinkler Strike

The city council in Guelph passed a bylaw in 2003 that was meant to counter the misuse of tap water. The law states that watering lawns in the rain is verboten, which means that if it looks like rain, residents had better remember to switch off their automatic sprinkler systems. Sprinkler water that runs off lawns and into streets will also garner a visit from a bylaw officer, as will water hoses that are found leading to swimming pools. Residents who don't comply can have the amount of water supplied to their homes reduced.

Hosers

Residents in the town of Milton who wish to water their lawns or gardens must, according to municipal bylaw, do so with a hose because the use of sprinklers is forbidden, except for new grass plantings, for which a permit is required.

Promoting Well-being

Atikokan has a bylaw called "Bulk Water Sales" that effectively puts the town's fire department water-pumpers to work delivering water to residents who have dried-up wells. For a $200 fee, a tanker will arrive, fill up the well and leave homeowners smiling. It's a good idea—almost. The delivered water arrives, all right, but it comes with a statement that it's not potable, and that it's up to consumers to make it drinkable.

Stay out of the Water

The Water Feature Bylaw of 2001 that was passed by Waterloo prohibits the introduction of any living organism into rivers, lakes or streams on municipal property. "Living organism" is a bit ambiguous, so maybe it just means "people keep out, and dogs, too"?

Tantalizing Taps

The supply infrastructure that keeps Ottawa's citizens supplied with clean drinking water costs taxpayers over $1 billion, with an annual maintenance price tag of $121 million. Polls, however, revealed that over 47 percent of Ottawa residents consume bottled water only. In 2010, Ottawa's city council addressed the problem by budgeting $1.1 million for tap-water promotion, an endeavour that included the replacement of public drinking fountains that were originally removed to favour bottled-water vending machines.

Fooling With Mother Nature

For in the true nature of things, if we rightly consider, every green tree is far more glorious than if it were made of gold and silver.

–Martin Luther, theologian

OUTDOOR LIFE

The Tree Museum

The Arboreal Emblem Act of 1990 is a law that designates the eastern white pine as Ontario's official tree—the same tree that was cut almost to extinction between the 17th and 19th centuries to make ship masts. Mature eastern white pine trees can grow to a height of 40 metres, but they became so rare that the British navy actually established mast reserves. By law, only British naval personnel were allowed to cut trees in Ontario's designated Royal Navy forest reserves, and transgressors were summarily executed.

Today, the once ubiquitous eastern white pine exists in only two stands of forest in Ontario. One such sanctuary is in Algonquin Park, and the other is in the Algoma Highlands Conservancy. Both are otherwise (unofficially) known as Ontario's tree museums.

Swiss Cheese and Gravel

The Ontario Aggregate Resources Act of 1990 requires the Ministry of Natural Resources (MNR) to regulate gravel pits and stone quarries with respect to digging and blasting processes and pollution threats. Road building requires aggregate (gravel, sand and slag), and if the material happens to be close by, so much the better because the cost-per-tonne of a project obviously mounts if haulage is involved. Disheartening is how much leeway the province of Ontario gives to road builders who are selecting their quarry sites. And, unfortunately for Ontarians, one of the most convenient spots for road construction companies to get their aggregates is the historic and geologically important Niagara Escarpment. Large road construction projects and their ongoing maintenance have a clustering effect on gravel pits, and companies often share a single road to cut costs. What this means is that a bunch of pits will start popping up in the same area, so that different companies can use the same road, rather than build new ones. Thanks to this practice, certain areas of the Escarpment, when viewed from the air, now resemble Swiss cheese. This pillaging of an Ontario geographical wonder flies in the face of the Aggregate Resources Act's controls and regulations, and is becoming more common because of government downsizing of the MNR and the effective lobbying of aggregate companies. Ontario needs good roads, but not at the expense of a natural marvel like the Niagara Escarpment.

The Swiss-cheese effect is actually noticeable all over Ontario, courtesy of hundreds of abandoned gravel pits. This marring of the landscape was supposed to be remedied by the use of a fund created by a government tax on gravel haulage, but in 1999, for unknown reasons, most of this fund was returned to aggregate companies.

Birds of a Feather

In the early 1970s, the indigenous-to-Ontario bird, the double-crested cormorant, almost became extinct because of DDT accumulations in the Great Lakes' fish stocks. Cormorants are large, extremely gregarious birds that roost on small islands in huge numbers, which, in the end, causes the flora of their homes to be completely destroyed, thanks to all the guano. Cormorants are also gluttons for fish, and commercial fishermen were not sad to see the bird's numbers dwindle. However, after DDT was banned in 1974, the cormorant made a remarkable recovery, and estimates put its numbers in Ontario at more than one million by 2010. Indeed, studies indicated everything was on track by 2006, when it was discovered that the number of cormorants was already unmanageable. Attempting to deal with the problem directly, Prince Edward–Hastings MPP Ernie Parsons put forth a private member's bill to amend the Fish and Wildlife Conservation Act to allow for the hunting of double-crested cormorants year-round in order to control their numbers. The bill didn't get passed because naysayer MPPs thought the bird deserved more study.

In 2008, the cormorant study continued while a colony of the incredibly foul-smelling birds set up shop near the Georgian Bay cottages of several influential MPPs. Suddenly, interest in studying the bird dwindled and another try was made at amending the Fish and Wildlife Conservation Act. Named Bill 62, it passed first reading and went to a committee before a second reading. The problem here is that nothing else happened, and Bill 62 has been continuously sidelined in the name of "more study." In 2010, with the study temporarily halted and Bill 62 stalled, the double-crested cormorant continues to be Ontario's own version of the locust plague.

Rabies on the Rise

Rabies, once the scourge of Ontario's red fox population, as well as a fearful disease for humans, has been all but eliminated by a concerted government effort that has included oral bait vaccinations and mass fox hunts. From 1953 to 2003, 58,000 rabid animals were reported to government agents, and most of them were red foxes and skunks infected with an Arctic fox variant of the disease. This variant has almost disappeared, thanks to the elimination program.

However, in 1999, a new type of rabies, the raccoon variant, was discovered in Ontario, and the number of reported cases has risen every year since. Raccoons are sociable animals, and prospects for a rabies epidemic like the one that once affected red foxes are, unfortunately, favourable. This is bad news for cities well-populated with raccoons. Estimates put Toronto's

raccoon population at around 750,000, and should rabies take hold, walking the dog after dinner will be a fond memory.

Ugly Is as Ugly Does

How a government treats the wildlife of its country, province or municipality is often a prime indicator of how that government treats its populace. A government that disregards wildlife is a one with little or no regard for its citizens, demonstrated by both the U.S. and Canadian governments when they allowed the 19th-century decimation of the plains buffalo, the main food source for half the population of both countries. Regrettably, in 2005, Ontario's Ministry of Natural Resources (MNR) put on an extremely ugly face once again when it seized a two-year-old doe from a couple who had saved her from certain death and then raised her. The doe, named Bam-Bam, was taken away because the law says people are not allowed to own wild animals.

Bruce Straby, the farmer who took the deer in, was essentially told "the deer can't be kept, she has to be let go or killed." In response, Straby was on the phone for weeks trying to get help from the government, but ended up getting nowhere. Then, in December 2006, the MNR showed up at the Straby farm with the police, and they took Bam-Bam away to be euthanized. Good fortune struck, however, when a zoo near Ottawa volunteered to take the deer. By then, the story had attracted the media's attention, and the public was outraged by the whole affair. This outrage turned to petitioning, and people began calling their MPPs, which prompted MPP Lisa MacLeod to say on the floor of the Ontario legislature that it might be a good exercise in public relations to give the Strabys a break. The Straby family got Bam-Bam back, along with a visit and an apology from Premier Dalton McGuinty.

WEIRD LAWS ABOUT FLORA AND FAUNA

Logging Loss

In 1988, the Temagami Wilderness Society focused public attention on the threat by loggers to some of Ontario's last old-growth forests. The pressure forced the government to cancel logging permits for those areas, and in 1994, the Ontario Environmental Assessment Board (OEAB) added old-growth forest conservation to its legally binding orders that the Ontario Ministry of Natural Resources (MNR) has to obey. The MNR is responsible for issuing clear-cut timber permits, and it paid no attention to the OEAB's decree, and since the board's orders didn't carry a penalty for contravention, the loggers have remained in Ontario's old-growth forests ever since.

Conservation Customs

Ontario has 36 conservation areas that protect over 135,000 hectares of land, and each conservation area has individual regulations that are stated under the Ontario Conservation Authorities Act. Most sets of the regulations contain 36 rules that encompass every illegal action imaginable, including begging. Visitors can't do anything in a conservation area without permission—swimming, boating, hiking or camping are all prohibited. Hunting game and training hunting dogs, however, are allowable actions that are covered by the Game and Fish Act.

Curbing the Conflagrations

The Township of Frontenac Islands is composed of Howe Island and Wolfe Island, two large and scenic islands located in the St. Lawrence River, where it is permissible through bylaw to burn leaves, brush and yard waste. The stipulation is

FOOLING WITH MOTHER NATURE

that landowners must first notify the fire department and be prepared to pay a fee of $350 per hour should a fire get out of control.

I Came Home and My Tree was Gone

Under the Toronto Municipal Code, Article 1, Section 813-1, is a bylaw that, with an owner's consent, allows for the inspection and removal of infected trees on public or private property. Toronto city council must have had second thoughts, though, because Section 813-2 now exists, and it states the same regulation as Section 813-1, except the words "owner's consent" are missing. How convenient.

Geriatric Greenery

Toronto is serious about mature trees, and cutting one down on private property without first obtaining a permit will net the property owner a $1000 fine for every felled tree.

Crazy Cutting

The Trees Act of Ontario allows utility workers to cut down any tree they need to. In 2006, along Granite Lake near Kenora, hydro workers gave the chop to a giant red pine to facilitate running a power line to a lakeside cottage. A slice of that tree was sent to provincial arborists, who confirmed that it was over 500 years old.

The Trees are Sick

The Injury or Destruction of Trees Bylaw is the weird title of a tree-cutting regulation in Mississauga, Aurora and several other Ontario municipalities. According to the bylaw, after a person applies for a permit and is approved, they can cause the injury or destruction of up to five trees, but only after submitting an arborist's report on the health of those trees and displaying a sign of intent to injure or destruct the trees.

The permit fee is $415, and objections from the public can result in the denial of a permit.

The Domino Effect

In Oshawa, it's illegal to climb trees. The establishment of this bylaw was a knee-jerk reaction by city council to protect themselves against lawsuits after a boy fell from a tree that was located on city property. Taking a cue from Oshawa, many other Ontario municipalities have enacted bylaws that also make it illegal to climb, wade, swing or, so it seems, do anything physical on public property and in parks. In fact, in Toronto, residents aren't supposed to do anything in public parks but walk, stand or sit. If they want to do something else, it needs to be in accordance with whatever is stated by signage, or else an authorized permit must be obtained. No picnics, no tossing a Frisbee, no balloons, no dogs, no bikes, no running, no anything except what's allowed by signage or permit. However, on one of Toronto Island's beaches, Hanlan's Point, everything seems to be allowed—beachgoers can even strip down and be one with nature, if they so choose.

Foliage Foibles

To liaison with the province's army of forest regulators, many Ontario municipalities, such as Stratford, have enacted a bylaw that allows for the appointment of a "tree commissioner." In other words, an arboreal cop who has the power to poke around in municipal and private woodlands and lay serious charges against offenders if an offence is discovered. For example, cutting down Christmas trees that grow on city property can garner offenders a fine of up to $50,000.

The Picnic Price

In Huntsville, having a picnic in the park costs residents $22, as stipulated in this town's Fees Bylaw of 2008. There's also no smoking, no beer, wine or liquor, no hugging or climbing trees—just finish the picnic, clean up and go home.

Soil Sentries

Bylaws requiring that topsoil be removed by permit are becoming more common, and kudos to the municipality of Central Manitoulin for being a pioneer in topsoil preservation. Topsoil is gold, and to waste any is practically equivalent to taking food from the mouths of Ontarians. Thankfully, central Manitoulin Island requires a permit to remove even a shovelful of topsoil, which, among other things, makes the community a jewel in Ontario's crown.

Lawn Liaisons

The Ontario Cosmetic Pesticides Ban Act of 2009 prohibits the use of pesticides and herbicides on lawns, gardens and walkways. However, the act allows for the use of glyphosate-based herbicides such as Monsanto's Roundup—a product that's available at almost every garden centre—for use on poisonous plants. Monsanto's Roundup and products like it are banned for use on lawns, but people are still buying large quantities anyway. Can it be that every yard in Ontario is suffering an outbreak of poison ivy?

Wild Weeds

Lawns improve when they're allowed to grow longer before being mowed. In London, Ontario, however, the city has a dim view of long grass, and residents who let their lawns grow over 3.8 centimetres will find city workers moving in to mow their lawns, and then leaving behind hefty fines. At the other end of the spectrum, municipalities such as Bruce Mines lump lawns and weeds together according to the "eight-inch (20-centimetre) rule"—any longer, and lawns will be cut and residents fined.

Say What?

In Pelam, in Niagara wine country, residents are required to keep their properties tidy courtesy of a "clean-yard bylaw" that contains the following head-scratcher: "Every owner, lessee or occupant shall keep his grounds, yard or vacant land filled up, drained, clean or cleared up."

Vindictive Vegetation

Toronto requires its residents to look after their residential streets, and it will turn a blind eye to the planting of a few flowers, but if vegetables or vegetable vines from an individual's garden stray onto a city street, he or she will receive a terse letter from the Ministry of Transportation that orders the vegetation's removal, post-haste. This seems like an odd attitude, considering the entire province is leaning more and more toward locally grown eats.

Butterfly Bearings

The Ontario Weed Control Act of 1990 is legislation that requires landowners to destroy all listed harmful weeds that are growing on their properties. Sadly, this act is also killing a great hero of the insect world, the monarch butterfly, because this most graceful continental traveller requires a listed noxious weed—the common milkweed—to host its larvae.

Puzzling Plastic

The Ontario Ministry of the Environment is presented every few years with a mystery when millions of white plastic pellets wash ashore on Lake Huron beaches during the fall months. It's assumed this phenomenon contravenes Ontario laws against pollution, and although the ministry has thoroughly investigated the incidents, it's still unable to pinpoint the source of this recurring threat that is most likely harmful to fish and wildlife.

Pet Protection

People in Ontario had better be kind to their pets because under Bill 50, a 2010 provincial amendment to the Ontario Society for the Prevention of Cruelty to Animals Act, a fine of up to $60,000 and a lifetime ban from owning pets can be levied against anyone caught being cruel to an animal. Giving pets the legal teeth to bite back at animal abusers is good legislation, but why did it take so long?

Triple Fail

In the cottage-country town of Bracebridge, if a dog escapes from its leash and dashes onto a beach and into the water, the owner is guilty of three bylaw offences—failure to keep a dog under control, failure to keep a dog from being at large and failure to keep a dog from a swimming area. The fine is $360. "But, your honour, the dog is only a teacup Yorkie!"

Pay Up

The town of Dryden arms its dogcatcher with a host of bylaws that can easily relieve residents of their hard-earned cash. All infractions are rewarded with $100 fines and include bad behaviour from cats, dogs and assorted other animals. The guidelines are actually pretty normal, except for one: "permitting a dog to scare a person." One surprise bark in Dryden, and a dog owner's pocketbook can be lighter by $100.

Vicious Verification

Speaking of dogs, if a canine bites a person or another dog in Goderich, the offending dog will be declared vicious, which means the owner is required to purchase third-party "vicious dog insurance" and display a vicious dog sign on the property where the animal is secured. The Goderich bylaw, however, fails to address any situation in which a dog owner refuses to buy insurance or post a sign.

Get a Leash

Losing a dog in Ontario can be a traumatic and financially disastrous experience for tourists, or anyone, for that matter. The Ontario Municipal Act grants municipalities a lot of leeway in the creation of their animal-control bylaws, and sometimes that means selling or killing Fido if he's not claimed within three days. That's the traumatic part. The financial disaster can occur when the pet owner goes to claim his or her dog, only to find out that it's being held for a ransom of expenses incurred, including a veterinarian's bill. Whether they need to or not, dogs are often sent to the vet for a complete physical, and owners get to go to the bank machine to pay the bill.

Bogus Burial

In many Ontario municipalities, it's against the law to bury a pet in the backyard. Okay, fine, Fido can go to a municipal pet cemetery. But in these times, how long did you think this practice would continue unopposed? In 2010, pet cemeteries came under attack by the Liberal government. It wants to disallow the pet cemeteries' tax-free status because, apparently, cemeteries are for burying human remains, period. If municipalities are forced to pay taxes on pet-cemetery properties, burial costs for the family cat/dog/hamster will obviously go up, and residents will likely return to performing backyard interments, laws be damned. Besides, what can a bylaw enforcement officer even do in this case? Obtain a warrant to dig up the bones of a cat?

Personal Zoos Restricted

The Respecting Animals Bylaw of 1990, passed by the town of Ingersoll, limits the number of pets allowed in a household. A resident can have two pets: a bird and a dog, a cat and a dog or any combination of these approved animals. If a resident is caught with more than two pets, the infraction can result in a $5000 fine. And just so everyone's clear, pet pythons over 60 centimetres in length are strictly forbidden and have to be killed, skinned and hung on the wall. Okay, not really. I had you there for a minute, didn't I?

Take Note
Gravenhurst has a bylaw that bans all pets except rats, cats, dogs, gerbils and...hedgehogs.

Out of Sight, Out of Mind
The town of Espanola, like many other Ontario municipalities, has a bylaw that prohibits the keeping of certain animals

within town limits. However, unlike other communities, Espanola does allow the ownership of horses and mules, and provides a subsection in its bylaw for the keeping of almost any fowl or animal imaginable as long as it's out of sight and no one complains about it. Common sense rules in Espanola.

Fertile Fido

In the town of Pickering, if a dog has a litter of puppies, they can be sold without any problems. However, should that dog procreate a second time, the owner is required to obtain a breeder's licence.

No Bread for Bears

Tired of begging bears and moose, the town council of Fort Frances passed a wildlife feeding bylaw that made it illegal to hand out food to any wild animal, save birds, squirrels and chipmunks. The little guys came out on top, while the big fellows were delegated to doing their panhandling on highways and in campgrounds.

Foul Fowl

Niagara Falls is blessed with a multitude of green spaces. Pheasants and rabbits abound, however, and hoping to cut down on their numbers, city council passed a bylaw that issued 200 hunting licences (for a fee of only $3.50 each) to 200 residents for the bagging of those species. This is perhaps an action Toronto should consider in aiming to reduce the raccoon population to at least a more tolerable 500,000.

Rurally
Weird

*I think it pisses God off if you walk by the color purple in
a field somewhere and don't notice it.*

—Alice Walker, *The Color Purple*

COUNTRY LIVIN'
Farm Fresh

At the turn of the 20th century, 75 percent of Ontarians lived on farms, and 100 years later, that figure reversed itself, with only 25 percent of the province's people living the rural life. For some, however, that might not be as idyllic as it sounds. Corporate behemoths have eclipsed many family farms, and they are now agricultural dynamos that contribute $25 billion to the Ontario economy and employ more than 650,000 people collectively.

It seems like the soul has been burned out of farming, and although food production has increased tenfold in half a century, that expansion has been, for the most part, dictated by government-sanctioned marketing boards that limit the choices of consumers in the grocery store. Sixty percent of Ontarians buy their food from grocery stores where they choose from four or five kinds of apples, two or three types of pears, four varieties of tomatoes, four potato breeds, two cucumber strains and whatever else ships best and has a long shelf life. Eggs come out of cold storage, dairy products from factories, and daily breads are full of preservatives and unpronounceable ingredients. In the face of this, it's little wonder that Ontarians are departing from the beaten path and planting their own gardens, buying organic foods and searching out heritage foods—the produce Ontarians enjoyed before big business took control.

Donkeys to the Rescue

The Livestock, Poultry and Honey Bee Protection Act of 1990 stipulates that municipalities must compensate farmers for losses as a result of predation by wolves, coyotes, dogs or foxes. At its inception, this act was hardly a concern because

predation was a rare occurrence. However, in 1995, coyotes began turning up in Ontario in ever-increasing numbers. The hungry coyotes ate anything, but preferred lamb. Going forward, municipal payments for lamb and sheep predation skyrocketed. Affected communities turned to the Ontario Ministry of Agriculture to help remedy the problem. In no time, the fix was in, courtesy of Alberta Agriculture and Rural Development—400-pound donkeys. Gotta love those western cowboys. Who else would think of using donkeys to guard sheep? But guard they do as they become part of the flock and end up keeping it safe because of the donkey's inborn dislike of dogs or any animal with canine attributes, including wolves, coyotes and foxes. A guard donkey in a flock of sheep is such a weird visual that it has become a tourist attraction of sorts, but visitors are advised to leave Fido at home because donkeys have been known to crash through fences and attack innocent-bystander dogs.

Poop Police

The Nutrient Management Act of 2002 is a provincial statute that regulates livestock manure in existing farm operations that produce an excess of 300 nutrient units. What is a nutrient unit? It's the amount of daily poop generated by one beef cow, 1.8 milk cows or 2.5 hogs. What farmers do with this, ummm, nutrient has to be stipulated on an application that's submitted to the Ontario Ministry of Agriculture, Food and Rural Affairs for approval. Anyone who's considering moving to the country to raise livestock for which the building of stables or a barn is required must also seek approval from the ministry when applying for a building permit, if they think the nutrient units produced on their farm will exceed five. Applicants have to supply all the particulars, including how the manure will be stored and where it will ultimately end up.

One can't help but wonder how the Ontario government came up with the term "nutrient management." Consultants, probably, and the decision most likely cost taxpayers a pretty penny. There is more to this act, too—"the disposal of dead stock regulation" that promotes the composting of dead livestock, which is a good deal for farmers because it saves them having to pay a renderer's pickup fee. It's a bad deal for renderers, though, because dead-stock pickups have dropped off considerably, forcing many out of business.

Killing the Buzz

The Bees Act of 2006 is legislation that provides for the licensing, inspection and reporting by apiarists when any transactions involving honeybees are conducted. Keeping a few hives on-site—once a farm tradition—is now so rife with bureaucratic red tape and bee police that apiarists are few and far between, and good honey has become an expensive luxury in Ontario. So acute is the honey shortage that some favourite Ontario honey brands (that will remain nameless) are cutting their product with cheap imported honey.

Read labels carefully, and buy only 100 percent Ontario honey to support those gutsy apiarists who persevere.

A Nasty Surprise

Rural property owners in northern or southeastern Ontario, or those contemplating the purchase of rural property in these areas, should be aware of the parameters of ownership. In Ontario, when it comes to property, there is two-dimensional surface area, which can be seen and measured, and the third dimension, which is the subsurface soil that lies underground and isn't often thought about until a crew shows up and wants to excavate or drill the property for minerals. "You can't do that! This is private property, my property!"

Not so. The crew's foreman can present a property owner with a permit the company bought from the province giving him carte blanche to dig or drill into the subsurface, which is technically owned by the province of Ontario. In Ontario, subsurface rights trump surface rights, and property owners are denied legal redress. To add salt to the wound, mining crews can leave their mess for the land owner to clean up. Worse yet, if anything of value is found, the property owner won't receive a cent because all royalties will be paid to the subsurface owner, the Ontario government. It's a nasty business, and an unfair one, because in 1997, the Mike Harris Conservative government created and passed Bill 68, which was legislation that transferred subsurface rights from the provincial government to landowners in the southwest of the province. However, that left the remainder of Ontario, where any hidden minerals of value on "private" property are up for grabs by prospectors.

WEIRD FACTS ABOUT RURAL LIFE

Crappy Compost

Ontario's Dead Animal Disposal Act of 2006 allows for the composting of dead cows and horses on a farm, but the animals have to be covered by at least 60 centimetres of a material that's high in carbon—corncob husks, sawdust or animal bedding. Urbanites visiting farms should be warned of the occasional stench, and to not get too close to giant compost piles.

Bedevilled by Beavers

The Ontario Drainage Act sanctions the removal of beaver dams from natural and private drainage channels and ditches, but it puts landowners in a dammed-if-we-do and damned-if-we-don't situation. Under the act, property owners are legally accountable for flooding caused by the removal of beaver dams. But, if property owners don't remove the obstructing beaver dam, the act also holds them responsible for up-channel flooding. Damn those dams!

Manure Manoeuvres
The Farming and Food Production Protection Act of 1998 is legislation designed to protect farmers from nuisance suits brought by owners of properties near agricultural land. Before this law's enactment, when farmers laid down the spring manure, it meant a full calendar for Ontario courts, and the issue took up valuable time that was better spent on more serious issues.

Fleeing the Coop
The Ontario Pounds Act of 1990 is a law that allows a municipal pound keeper to lock up escaped livestock and poultry. The subsequent recovery of property damaged by the escapees is also outlined within this law. And do you remember Ontario's fence viewers? The Pounds Act provides for the appeal of damages to Ontario's fence viewers. Gotta love those fence viewers—they're everywhere!

Sick
in Ontario

You can die of the cure before you die of the illness.

–Michael Landon, actor

HEALTH-CARE CONUNDRUMS

Doctors Wanted

During Dalton McGuinty's 2007 election campaign, he looked directly at the TV camera and swore he would address Ontario's acute shortage of trained medical personnel by hiring 9000 nurses by 2012. He promised the same thing in the 2008 budget, but by 2010, only about 20 percent of the promised 9000 were employed, and young nursing students who invested heavily in their education based on his promise in 2007 were having trouble finding jobs in Ontario. Unfortunately, for the province, it's no secret that many of its nurses are leaving to work in other parts of Canada or in the U.S.

Ontario is also suffering from a shortage of doctors, especially in northern communities. The College of Physicians and Surgeons of Ontario is the medical licensing authority in the province, and it certifies about 3000 doctors per year. About 40 percent of those doctors are foreign-trained, which is an improvement over the five percent of a few years ago, but still, it's not enough to prevent the deterioration of a great medical system. Easing the licensing restrictions for the several thousand international medical-school graduates who want to work in Ontario could easily reverse the deficit. In order to make this happen, politicians need to keep their promises, and the government needs set up special training hospitals to help internationally trained doctors become more quickly certified in Ontario. Foreign-taught doctors automatically pass all the medical exams, but in order to become a physician in the province, they also need to complete a residency in a hospital. They can't do that, however, unless they have gone through previous training at an Ontario hospital. The problem is that there are only a few hundred openings at training hospitals within the province, which is bitterly laughable because hospitals all over Ontario are in dire need of new doctors.

Old and Happy in Port Hope
Port Hope's town council has discovered a cure for all ills, and in 2010, put it in writing with a bylaw it calls the "Leisure Services Master Plan." According to Port Hope folks, plenty of leisure combats diabetes, cancer, heart disease, respiratory illness, stress and depression, and it contributes to emotional well-being. The Master Plan is the result of

a carefully thought out, long-range strategy meant to attract senior citizens away from Toronto to Port Hope. And why not? Doing nothing in Port Hope will alllow people to live long and happy—thanks to the bylaw, it's practically guaranteed!

The Peter and Paul Effect

The Ontario Ministry of Health and Long-Term Care is mandated by the government to look after the health of Ontarians, but according to provincial ombudsman Andre Marin, people's health is something the government has been neglecting, especially with regard to the long-term care of the elderly, as well as wait times for serious surgical procedures. Ontario's ombudsman has a staff of 50, with 24 investigators, and Marin's team found that despite the Ontario government's 1997 investment of $100 million into long-term care, Ontario's elderly have received little benefit, and problems with the province's nursing homes abound. However, reports from Marin have prodded the health ministry into actions that have shortened the wait times for some medical procedures in the province's hospitals. Wait times in 2010 for priority procedures such as cancer surgery, hip and knee replacements, radiation therapy, cataract surgery and diagnostic imaging are shorter, on average, by about 35 percent. Unfortunately, the tables have only just turned, and the reduction has been at the expense of other procedures and elective surgeries, many of which now have extended wait times. Taking from Peter to pay Paul is an old trick, but it doesn't seem so funny when Peter is the one waiting for his pacemaker to be put in place.

Wi-Fi Hysteria

In 2006, in response to information that Wi-Fi radiation might be harmful, Lakehead University in Thunder Bay banned Wi-Fi from its campus, despite Health Canada's insistence that school Wi-Fi networks are safe. The Ontario Agency for Health Protection and Promotion, a government agency formed in 2007 to provide better hospital and public communication after the SARS fiasco, took on the task of reviewing all available scientific data, and on September 16, 2010, it released a report that recognized a link between cellphone use and cancer, but also corroborated Health Canada's position that Wi-Fi networks emit lower levels of radiation that are probably harmless to students.

In 2010, in response to the spreading hysteria about the effects of Wi-Fi networks on children, parents with kids at St. Vincent-Euphrasia Elementary School, in Meaford, voted to ban Wi-Fi from the school, despite continued assurances from the municipal council and Health Canada that the networks are harmless. Municipal school boards across the province are also concerned, and investigations are likely to cause many others to follow the Meaford school's example.

Bacterial Time Bombs

In Ontario, the Ministry of Public Health and Long-Term Care is responsible for forewarning hospitals in the province when there is an infectious disease threat to the public. This includes threats similar to the severe acute respiratory syndrome (SARS) outbreak in 2003, which garnered for the city of Toronto the appellation "SARS City." And, according to a 2007 report released by an investigating commission, the finger was pointed at authorities who lacked the appropriate communication, blurred their power and failed to heed the advice of front-line health-care workers, all of which created a situation that ran counter to the spirit of the law that created the ministry.

The ministry fared better during the 2010 H1N1 outbreak, but it still came up short of vaccine. Both SARS and H1N1 are expected to return every few years because of the high amount of airline traffic interchange between Canada and Asia, the main source of infectious breakouts of this type. Luckily, though, when an epidemic occurs in southeastern Ontario, residents can now track the spread of the infectious disease and thus avoid contaminated areas through a computer-mapping tool called "Infection Watch Live," an adaptation of a U.S. program that tracks potential terrorist-spread threats such as anthrax. To watch is to be forewarned, but a better initiative is for Ontario's authorities to simply quarantine the source when an outbreak first occurs.

WEIRD LAWS ABOUT ONTARIO'S HEALTH

Airing Things Out

Ontario has air-quality problems that are thought to affect the public's health, and even though the province does have the Clean Water Act, it has no legislation regarding air quality. Instead, it relies on the federal government's all-encompassing Environmental Protection Act of 2000 for guidance. This act is not specific legislation for clean air, but the Ontario government is still vitally interested in healthy skies and has taken to hiring expensive consultants to study the matter. A 2009 study in Oakville identified four areas of concern: industry, vehicle emissions, residential and…miscellaneous?

Drugstore Diagnosis

Drug-dispensing machines will soon be turning up in Ontario pharmacies. The province's minister of health has introduced legislation to permit their installation, and newspaper rumour has it that these potential money-makers are compensation meant to make up for the loss that pharmacies experienced after the decline of the lucrative tobacco business. Pharmacies, however, while still earning dispensing fees, will also have to make do with one less pharmacist. Buy a chocolate bar, buy a pop, buy medication?

Savings for the Sick

In Toronto, and in some other Ontario municipalities such as Brampton and Oshawa, city employees are allowed to bank up to 18 sick days per year, which they can then cash out at half-value upon retirement.

Blinded by the Light

Studies have proved that the bright lights in shopping-mall and strip-mall parking lots can adversely affect the health of Ontarians by interrupting their sleep patterns. Taking this into account, Richmond Hill's town council passed its Light Pollution Bylaw to regulate illumination levels and the hours of the outdoor lighting's operation, actions meant to provide relief to residents who have been living in the glare.

Money
Management

The law gives a dog more rights than the person he bites.

–J.C. McRuer, former Ontario Chief Justice

CENTS AND SENSIBILITY

The Tax Man

Before 1917, the collection of personal taxes was a municipal affair, but when the federal government took over the task, communities left with seriously depleted revenue had to conjure up new taxes, which often included labour taxes. Some northern Ontario mining towns collected the labour tax from mineworkers until the middle of the 20th century. Miners aside, working people throughout Ontario also became used to having their wages taxed, as there has always been some form of tax being charged in Ontario.

Fast-forward to 1999, when the provincial government had a balanced budget and surplus funds, and handed back to municipalities the responsibility of dealing with provincial, non-criminal transgressions, including highway traffic and liquor offences, and minor crimes against fish and wildlife. This change was a virtual goldmine that harkened back to old times, and there were almost limitless growth possibilities for community courts.

To facilitate that growth, Ontario municipalities took a page from history and adopted the 17th-century royal practice of sharing their tax booty with agents of the Crown. What this means in modern times is that "agencies" of municipalities, such as police and fire services, dogcatchers and bylaw enforcement officers, are expected to contribute to municipal salary and pension costs by using the infamous ticket-quota system. Is it for a resident's benefit that firemen come knocking to check smoke alarms, or is it that the firemen are out hunting, because in most Ontario municipalities, the ticket for an inoperative alarm is around $200? Additionally, in most municipalities, police officers are paid time and a half for appearing as witnesses for traffic tickets they have written, which is a powerful incentive for officers to write more tickets. Scenarios such as these can be questioned at almost every turn.

User Pays

During Ontario's formative years, from the mid-18th century to the mid-19th century, when both local government and private individuals built projects that benefited the public, the builders demanded a user fee, or tax. For example, toll roads and bridges were common, and residents paid a fee to use them. When farmers took grain to a mill to be ground into flour, they paid the road and bridge tolls there and back in hard cash. A jug of whiskey or a bottle of wine also came with a built-in government tax, as did tobacco and paraffin or whale oil for lighting.

In 1791, the Ontario government, then the Upper Canada government, instituted the Assessment Act, which was a tax on real estate and personal property. If a resident earned an income or owned anything of value, be it a house, horse, wagon or property, the government taxed it, and back then, the taxman was often the local justice of the peace or a county sheriff. In 1850, the Assessment Act was revised to exclude the taxation of personal property and income under $300, and the tax was instead concentrated on business accoutrements such as ships, store inventories, freight wagons and properties, the latter a vilified tax that has persisted until now. But why is property tax so reviled? Well, the reason is because its collection is based on a formula that doesn't take into account the ability to pay or benefits received, and monies collected under this tax can be used to support services that have nothing to do with property. This means the money goes toward helping the provincial and federal governments do...who knows what.

Today, Toronto collects around $2.6 billion in property taxes, and it keeps only six percent of that, with most of it going to the salaries of essential services personnel such as police, firefighters and sanitary workers. Yet, Toronto is still cash-strapped and has had to let its own property infrastructure deteriorate; roads need work, the sewer system is inadequate and bridges need repairing. So what are Toronto's politicos doing about the situation? They're talking about a new plan, and it's called user fees, which means toll roads and bridges and pay-by-the-pound garbage pickup. What goes around comes around.

It Takes Some Nerve

In 1996, the Public Sector Salary Disclosure Act was passed by the Mike Harris Conservative government to make the public sector more accountable to taxpayers. Unfortunately for the government, the Public Sector Salary Disclosure Act also required that the names of provincial and municipal government employees making over $100,000 annually be published, and since 1996, thanks to that document (dubbed the annual "sunshine list" by the media), inquisitive reporters have found countless discrepancies and suspicious activities.

For instance, in 2010, most Ontario residents were outraged when the Dalton McGuinty government released that year's sunshine list, which revealed that 63,671 of Ontario's civil servants earned a salary of more than $100,000. Over 2000

City of Toronto employees were on the list, with Toronto Transit Commission (TTC) drivers leading the parade. However, these people were pale soup when compared to the people in charge of Ontario's money rivers. Executive salaries at the LCBO, Ontario Power Generation and hospitals were through-the-roof ludicrous, sometimes approaching and surpassing $500,000 per year. In light of the populace's outrage, the Liberals made a public confession and promised to stop misleading citizens. And yet...

During a time of high unemployment rates and financial upheaval, Ontario working families in 2010 averaged an annual income of about $70,000. Not bad, but still peanuts in comparison to what some of the province's public servants raked in for what many see as the ability to make mistakes. Say that someone is a computer consultant who's making $2700 per day. Most people in this position would not have the audacity to bill their breakfast to the company that's paying them this huge amount of money. However, if that company was an agency of Ontario called eHealth, which creates electronic health records for Ontario residents, someone might decide to suffer a momentary lapse of judgment.

The predecessor to eHealth, the Smart Systems for Health Agency, burned through $647 million of taxpayers' money without producing a workable system, and nobody at Queen's Park seemed to care. Smart Systems was simply shut down and another venture was started—eHealth. It followed the same path as Smart Systems, and in 2010, Ontario auditor-general Jim McCarter announced that $1 billion of taxpayers' money had gone out the window for nothing. Heads rolled, and people got fired for, of all things, calling attention to the fiasco or for acting as scapegoats by deflecting attention away from negligent government store-minders. Reports that go into further detail are available online, and readers will be flabbergasted. But don't worry—the people who lost their jobs didn't lose any personal money. For example, even though she was part of the scheme that wasted $1 billion tax dollars, fired eHealth boss Sarah Kramer walked away from the debacle with a year's salary worth $380,000, a severance of $317,000 and a bonus of $114,000—all despite being on the job for less than a year. Also implicated was Ontario Deputy Health Minister Ron Sapsford, who resigned after reporters discovered his yearly salary of almost $500,000 was being funnelled through a Hamilton hospital in order to skirt the government's own salary cap.

A much larger problem is going to present itself down the road, though, when the sunshine boys and girls dip into Ontario's tax dollars to finance their pensions, most of which are pegged at 70 percent of their salaries. Readers doing the math might be changing occupations as we speak, hoping to hop onto the civil gravy train.

Ontario's Eco Tax Fiasco

On July 1, 2010, Ontario's Liberal government debuted a tax on retail products, such as paint and antifreeze, deemed toxic to the environment. For Ontarians, it was time to welcome the introduction of the infamous eco tax, which was, according to Minister of Environment John Gerretsen, "not a tax, but a fee meant to offset the costs of recycling." The province's recycler, Stewardship Ontario, is a not-for-profit company formed under the quasi-government-and-industry-run Waste Diversion Act, and it collects money from businesses that sell eco-"unfriendly" products, Canadian Tire and Home Hardware among them. Stewardship Ontario then gives most of that money to municipalities for their blue-box programs, keeping approximately one-third to fund various studies and management tasks, and to meet payroll. In the end, municipalities actually end up with double the money because they already collect property tax for recycling purposes, so which costs, exactly, are being "offset" by the eco fee?

In an effort to further increase "eco" revenue, the government upped the tax, as well as expanded the list of items to be taxed to a whopping 9000 and increased the types of businesses that were to charge it. It was fully expected that retailers would continue to add the tax into retail prices, but that failed to happen because business owners instead included an extra line on their receipts for the fee, with many tacking on a handling charge. Consumers went crazy. The eco fee, labelled a "stealth tax" by the media, created such a backlash that it lasted all of four weeks. The tax did, however, manage to bring in a cool $100 million.

WEIRD LAWS ABOUT TAXES AND FEES

The Paying Public

Elliot Lake's town council has embraced user fees whole-heartedly, and, as such, every municipal space is available for rent. Skating rinks, beaches, community centres, swimming pools, fire halls, parks—if the town owns it, people can rent it. Elliot Lake will even rent space in its cemetery if someone needs to store a loved one for reburial somewhere else. The cost? Fifty dollars per month. User fees such as these have been adopted by many Ontario municipalities, and some have completely forgone metering and monthly billing in favour of charging a flat fee for water, sewage and garbage pickup services.

Troublesome Taxes

The Stronger City of Toronto for a Stronger Ontario Act of 2006 is legislation that is meant to provide Toronto with new powers to regulate and collect taxes and fees. This was like giving candy to a baby because, suddenly, Toronto had a list of new items to be taxed and regulated, and that list included everything from theatre tickets to vehicle licence renewals to property transfers. Two taxes were immediately implemented, though—the land transfer tax and the personal vehicle registration tax. User fees were also introduced for garbage collection and plastic bags, and regulations that governed vehicle emissions were put in place as well. The results were predictable as businesses began to pull up stakes and move to areas that were more tax friendly. Citizens began yelling, "Not a cent more!" so loudly that in 2010, during the Toronto mayoral election, out went the old regime and in came the new, which many hope will be more responsive to businesses and taxpayers.

Ontario
Show Biz

If you can't dazzle them with brilliance, baffle them with bull.

–W.C. Fields, comedian

ENTERTAINMENT OF THE ERAS

What Do You Want to Do Tonight?

In the 1700s and 1800s, life in Ontario was about as exciting as watching crows in a cornfield—aside from the odd bash-up with the U.S., of course. Ontarians attended church on Sundays, participated in weddings, funerals and barn raisings and, as macabre as it sounds, hangings were a source of entertainment. A public hanging meant that schools, stores and taverns were closed, and the entire countryside was brought in for a scaffold picnic where arriving early meant a good view of a dropped and dancing body. These crowds also attracted itinerant "medicine shows" that prolonged the excitement by peddling high-alcohol-content medicines laughingly called "snake oil" by imbibers. These wagon shows eventually became small rail-travelling circuses that grew in size and frequency as the railway was laid down farther and father north and west of Toronto.

As cities grew, so did entertainment venues. For adults, there were magic lantern shows that featured hand-painted slides projected by an arc lamp onto a large white sheet, and for families, there were small amusement parks. The men, of course, had their burlesque shows. Entertainers in these times were always attempting daring feats to attract the paying public, and one of the highlights of the later 19th century was to see the Great Blondin walk on a wire suspended over Niagara Falls. He actually became so good at this feat that during a few of his many spectacular crossings, he carried a lit grill on his back, stopped halfway across, cooked lunch or breakfast and then lowered the food down to spectators on the *Maid of the Mist* boat. Now that's show biz.

As the 20th century rolled around, magic lantern shows morphed into moving picture shows, small amusement parks grew massive and tiny dancing rooms became grand dance halls where crowds gathered to listen to the music of the big bands.

Now, in the early 21st century, people still love to be entertained, but lawsuits, paranoia and insurance have neatly put a cap on, and in some cases stopped completely, many of the public's sources of early recreation.

Barrelling Over Niagara Falls

So you want to launch yourself over Niagara Falls in a barrel and join the ranks of the approximately 17 other daredevils who have either succeeded or died attempting the big drop before you? Well, you can't undertake this feat without written authorization from the Niagara Parks Commission, and it has never, nor will it likely ever, put pen to paper to produce such a document. The bylaw, however, hasn't stopped intrepid souls who have opted to ignore authority, and then pay the $10,000 fine and perhaps spend a few weeks in jail if they survived. Wirewalkers, on the other hand, have had more success in obtaining permission to conquer the falls, but few of them have actually applied for and been granted access, even though the chances of surviving a walk across the falls on a wire are a lot better than choosing to go over courtesy of the time-honoured barrel trick. But if you can't walk a tightrope? No problem. Just find someone who can and hitch a ride. The Great Blondin provided this service, after all, piggybacking his manager on one crossing.

Walking on Water

Niagara Falls used to freeze over, forming an "ice bridge," and before 1912, people ventured out onto the Niagara River's ice and observed the frozen falls at an awe-inspiring angle. In fact, one day in February 1888, as many as 20,000 people stood on the ice while musicians played, people tobogganed and residents drank liquor and beer in hastily constructed shanties. People continued to walk freely on the ice every year until the winter of 1912, when the ice bridge heaved once, broke in two and dropped three tourists into the icy water. A bylaw was passed immediately that declared it illegal to venture out onto the Niagara Falls ice. No matter now, because the ice bridge across Niagara Falls is only found in the history books, thanks to global warming.

Elvis Everywhere

In Collingwood, in 2001, city council passed a bylaw that outlined rules and operating procedures for what had grown from a minor celebration to a major event, the Collingwood Elvis Festival. The festival had broken annual attendance records during each year of its existence, and it's no wonder because this four-day, Graceland-sanctioned event is a hoot, with parades, concerts, beach parties, plenty of fried peanut butter and banana sandwiches and over 100 Elvis impersonators. In Collingwood, Elvis is definitely in the building, whether he's crooning onstage or combing his hair in his dressing room. Sure, it's true that Elvis, the man, is gone, but his legislated spirit sure does live on in Collingwood.

Again with the Blue Plaques

The Ontario Heritage Trust (OHT) is a government agency that was formed by the Ontario Ministry of Culture to acquire and maintain properties and buildings of historical importance within the province. The trust's inventory is considerable: 24 heritage sites, such as Uncle Tom's Cabin, the Elgin and Winter Garden Theatre Centre and the Enoch Turner Schoolhouse, and over 140 historic estates that include more than 100 tracts of land necessary for the protection of wildlife, wetlands, Carolinian forests and more. The trust, however, is probably best known to Ontarians for its blue-toned, bronze plaques that are mounted all over the province, wherever something of historical or cultural significance occurred.

The OHT is further responsible for the Premiers' Gravesites Program. It will be placing and maintaining the same blue-coloured plaques next to every Ontario premier's grave, but the plaques will also be draped with both the Ontario and Canadian flags.

The trust is Ontario's conservator of historical buildings as well, and although its mandate is to preserve these historical sites and operate them as museums that are open to the public, it also rents out these same attractions for private or corporate functions, as well as for filmmaking.

Scratch a Friendship

In Ontario, it should be no surprise that an IOU for a gambling debt is worthless in the eyes of the law. The Ontario Lottery and Gaming Corporation Act, however, does admit that the sharing of lottery tickets among friends or workmates creates a legal grey area, should there be a winning pick. If there is a dispute, lottery officials grill the winners as to the legality of possession, and payment is postponed until the courts settle proof of ownership. Few things break up relationships faster than a sudden windfall, and everyone from ex-spouses, to common-law partners, to drinking buddies, to co-workers, to family members can come forward claiming that there was an agreement between them and the winner to share the cost and subsequent winnings of a lottery ticket or tickets. Combining resources to buy lottery tickets can still be a good idea, but to prevent the deal going sour, participants are advised to sign each ticket, so there's no question about who's entitled to the winnings.

Big Beach Biz

The Ontario government has been indirectly benefiting from the beach business since the mid-1800s, when burgeoning streetcar and railway companies began to create destination parks. More rails to amusement parks meant more jobs and a better economy, not to mention the fees charged for the leases on the land. Beaches were at one time a huge revenue stream for Ontario, and the province embraced the business whole hog.

In the waning years of the 19th century, spending the summer in a city such as Toronto was often unbearable. For a respite from the heat, wealthy residents packed up the kids and moved out to the Toronto Islands to stay at either a cottage or at the Hanlan Hotel, which was built in 1878 at Hanlan's Point by John Hanlan, father of world-famous rower

Ned Hanlan. In time, ferry service to the islands made the trip easier, as well as allowed for day-trip excursions. Concession stands began to sprout up, selling everything from popcorn to hot dogs, and to keep people entertained, a lacrosse and baseball stadium was constructed, along with various amusement rides such as the "steeplechase," which was the precursor to the roller coaster.

Torontonians loved Hanlan's Point and packed the place every summer. In 1886, Hanlan's Point planted gardens, as well as constructed a boardwalk, picnic areas and a fenced-in space for swimming. There was also a merry-go-round and a theatre, and newspapers began calling Hanlan's Point "Ontario's Coney Island." It put Toronto on the tourist map and was such a success that it started an epidemic of beach development. In 1888, the Crystal Beach Amusement Park opened on Lake Erie; in 1898, the Boblo Island Amusement Park debuted on Bois Blanc Island, near the mouth of the Detroit River; in 1906, the Scarboro Beach Amusement Park, a.k.a. White City, the most expensive amusement park to that date, opened to rave reviews; in 1907, Stanley Beach Park was founded in Port Stanley, and the list goes on.

Amusement parks proved to be exceedingly profitable for investors, and by 1920, Toronto wanted in on the action, so it dredged up sand from the bottom of Lake Ontario and built a beach on the lakeshore that fronted a farm named Sunnyside. In 1922, the city began leasing out concessions for rides and "red hots," the hot dog brand that was bought by E.P Taylor and sold through the famous Honey Dew stands and shops. Sunnyside was the nail in the coffin for Hanlan's Point, but even after raking in dough for years, Sunnyside, too, closed, in 1955.

Ice Cream, Palaces and Ontario Law

In Britain, moving-picture houses were called "odeons," but because admission was a nickel in North America, people here used to call movie theatres "nickelodeons." In 1906, the first permanent nickelodeon, the Theatorium, opened in Toronto. Not much of a place, the Theatorium's seats were hard and its flicks only lasted a few minutes, but it was always packed. This fact eventually caught the attention of an American concessionaire named Nathan L. Nathanson, who did business with the Scarboro Beach Amusement Park, and is credited with introducing Toronto to the ice cream cone. One look at the Theatorium, though, and Nathanson was ready for a new business venture. He had a knack for knowing what the masses wanted, and what they wanted at the time, even more than the Theatorium, was a grand experience—a movie palace. Nathanson had worked on the fringe of the movie business, and in 1916, he masterminded the creation of the Regent Theatre chain with the help of four investors, one of whom was millionaire investment dealer J.P. Bickell.

In 1918, the Regent chain was renamed Paramount Theatres, but it had no relationship to Adolph Zukor's U.S.-based Paramount theatres—that is, until Zukor attempted to buy into the Canadian action. He had previously offered to buy Jule Allen's and William Maxwell Aitken's (a.k.a. Lord Beaverbrook's) Famous Players chain but was rejected, which is why he turned to Nathanson with fists full of cash. Nathanson decided to partner with Zukor, and the two of them built more theatres, constructing them strategically close to Famous Players theatres. By showing first-run U.S. Paramount pictures, Nathanson eventually drove Famous Players into bankruptcy, and in 1923, he bought 35 of Famous Players' finest venues.

Six years later, in 1929, Nathanson attempted to buy out Zukor, but Nathanson was the one who ended up resigning. He wasn't done with show business, though, and turned to J. Arthur Rank, the owner of the British Odeon Cinemas. The men created a handshake deal, and Odeon Canada formed to distribute Rank's pictures in Canada, as well as build more theatres. The pair built some of the best movie houses in the country, and along the way, Nathanson also gathered independent theatres and small regional chains into the Odeon fold.

In the 1930s, the federal and provincial governments accused Nathanson of violating anti-trust laws, and although the case never went anywhere, Nathanson was hounded constantly. When his son Paul took over the business in the 1940s, the authorities were still persisting, so in 1946, the Nathansons sold Odeon to Rank while continuing to manage both Odeon and Famous Players in the province. These movie-house chains were a duopoly in Ontario, and between them, controlled the province's theatre industry. The men behind the industry also seemed bigger than life itself, or at least certainly larger than life on the big screen, and it's little wonder that during the 1950s, Paul Nathanson was one of Canada's wealthiest citizens.

WEIRD FACTS ABOUT ONTARIO ENTERTAINMENT

Paid to Punch

The Ontario Athletics Control Act of 2010 licenses participants in public boxing matches, as well as assures their health and drug-free status, and it also guarantees the payment of match officials. Boxing promoters who have a history of criminal associations or financial diddling are denied a licence under this act, and permits issued to promoters have to be accompanied by certified cheques so that payment to approved match officiators is assured. This law has effectively shut the door on organized crime's involvement in the sport of boxing. In the same breath, it also doomed the sport in some ways because, as they say, the baby was thrown out with the bathwater.

Movie Maxims
In 2005, the Ontario Film Classification Act was passed to provide for the rating of films deemed appropriate for public viewing. The act also allows "unsuitable" films to be seized, which is a bit of jackboot politics.

Casino Carousing
The Ontario Casino Corporation Act states that fines of up to $50,000 can be issued if underage players (those under 19 years old) are caught gambling in a casino. "Gee, dad, my allowance is only $20 a week. How will I ever pay you back?"

Explosive Entertainment

The Ontario Explosives Act allows municipalities to declare certain days "firecracker days," and although most only designate Victoria Day and Canada Day as such, some are choosing to light up the night sky to celebrate everything from a founders' day to a winter fest. Properly handled and supervised, fireworks are fun, but, unfortunately, the prohibitionists have started to nag Ontario politicians for a complete ban on the sale of fireworks. If the hounding continues, it is almost inevitable that the government will cave in.

Big Top Ban

Tired of being entertainment brokers for its residents, the town council in Newmarket passed a "carnival bylaw" in 2009 that contains so many restrictive requirements for a permit that no circus would ever be foolish enough to apply.

Toiling
in Ontario

If it's your job to eat a frog, it's best to do it first thing in the morning. And if it's your job to eat two frogs, it's best to eat the biggest one first.

–Mark Twain, author and humourist

WORKED TO THE BONE

A Shock to the System

During the 18th and 19th centuries, when the Industrial Revolution was taking wing in Britain, Ontario, for the most part, remained a backwater province with the forestry industry as its main employer. Ontarians farmed, chopped trees, wove wool or kept shop—and that was all she wrote. To be profitable, factories needed a plentiful, cheap supply of coal, and since Ontario was not blessed with any deposits of that mineral, the province was stuck developmentally and was forced to buy manufactured products from the U.S. Toward the end of the 19th century, iron foundries using coal imported from the U.S. sprang up around small bog-iron deposits, but they only stayed in operation until the deposits ran out, and that was always quickly. It wasn't until beginning of the 20th century that Ontario discovered its industrial trump card—hydro electricity.

Minor Management

The Ontario Factories Act of 1884 (now the Occupational Health and Safety Act) was originally passed to ensure the safety and health standards of young workers in Ontario factories. It set the maximum hours of work at 10 hours a day and 60 hours per week for girls aged 14 to 16 and boys aged 12 to 14.

Death Dollars

Purchasing corporate-owned life insurance, or "dead peasants insurance," isn't a law of Ontario, but some might consider it corporate law, because most companies with large numbers of employees play this insurance game. What it means is that corporations simply insure all employees (without their knowledge) against death, and then collect the money should their demise occur on the job, at home or anywhere else.

The Government Grind

Since coming to power in 2003, Ontario's Liberal government has swelled the ranks of the public sector by one-third. Over one million Ontarians now wet their whistle at the public trough, and this is an absurd but fortuitous number for the Liberals at election time because people are usually loath to bite the hand that feeds them. Can a "never the twain shall meet" type of government provide effective rule for Ontarians, and can it afford the cost of finding out?

Education

An educated people can be easily governed.

–Frederick the Great, former king of Prussia

ATTENTION, CLASS

Ouch

A 1912 regulation of the Ontario Ministry of Education reads as follows:

> *In the case of French-speaking pupils who are unable to speak and understand the English language well enough for the purposes of instruction and communication, the following provision is hereby made: As soon as the pupil enters the school he shall begin the study and use of the English language.*

It seems a bit harsh, but it reflects the common attitude of Ontario educators for the next five decades—learn as directed or suffer the consequences. For boys, that doctrine, unfortunately, often involved the dreaded strap.

Peer Learning

In 2010, Ontario's Minister of Education, Leona Dombrowsky, backed the Greater Essex County District School Board's traditional approach to education by age. Case in point—an intelligent 10-year-old named Bachar Sbeiti, who was born in Montréal, was identified as being gifted at age three and sent off to a school for advanced children in Michigan. After graduating from grade eight, Bachar and his mother returned to live in Windsor, fully expecting that Bachar would start high school in grade nine. Instead, the Greater Essex County District School Board decided Bachar was to remain with his peers and was put back into grade five. Bachar and his mom were understandably upset. If the province doesn't recognize and nurture brilliance from a young age, where will that eventually leave Ontario?

Sabrina's Law

Legislation that requires Ontario schools to identify and form a plan of action for students with anaphylaxis (an acute allergic reaction to foods or chemical additives) is called Sabrina's Law. This is a private member's bill named for Sabrina Shannon, a Pembroke student who succumbed to anaphylactic shock after consuming french fries in the school cafeteria. Neither she nor the cafeteria cooks knew the fries contained a milk derivative that Sabrina was allergic to, and once she was stricken, it took too long for staff to figure out what to do and to find the 13-year-old girl's EpiPen, an epinephrine injector that would have saved her life. Now, thanks to Sabrina's Law, schools know who is allergic to what, the foods those students can and can't eat and what to do if a student goes into anaphylactic shock.

Kindergarten Fiasco

The Full Day Early Learning Statute Law Amendment Act of 2010 states that full-day kindergarten attendance of children between the ages of four and six is mandatory. Full-day kindergarten will see implementation in 600 Ontario schools, with classes supervised by teachers, early childhood educators and early childhood educator assistants. Dalton McGuinty's Liberals allotted $1.5 billion for this project, with parents expected to cover any shortfall by paying a reasonable fee. With the program barely off the ground, the parents' contribution has proved inadequate, and the plan is already encountering financial difficulties. Schools have laid off educator assistants, increased class sizes and raised the "reasonable" fees. What is supposed to be childcare for working parents is now, in some cases, costing more than standard daycare. This is shaping up to be another taxpayer washout.

Get a Job

Ontario secondary schools are required, under a regulation of the Ontario Education Act, to hire at least one, and not more than three, student trustees from their complement of full-time students. The trustees receive $2500 for serving a full term. All students are eligible, except for those serving a sentence in a penal or correctional institution. What these students are expected to do is a mystery.

The Lunch Bunch

The Healthy Food for Healthy Schools Act of 2008 is meant to reduce or eliminate junk food from school lunch programs. "No pop, Twinkies, chips or fries, and kids will thank us," is the mindset, but as any youngster knows, the effort ain't worth squat, because students who want a Twinkie (and have access to junk food at home) will simply bring it to school.

Midnight
Herring

*When I sell liquor, it's called bootlegging; when
my patrons serve it on Lake Shore Drive,
it's called hospitality.*

–Al Capone, gangster

ADVENTURES IN CONTRABAND

Smuggling as Necessity

During Ontario's early years as a province, its money arrived from Britain. The coins were minted from precious metals— the pounds from silver and the guineas, or sovereigns, from gold. This hard currency, which was sent over in crates, was subject to weather delays, the sinking of ships and piracy. If the money failed to arrive, the government issued scripts, or hand-signed promissory notes, that were redeemable in gold or silver. This was all well and good, but at the same time, the government insisted that residents pay their taxes in hard currency, no scripts allowed. This policy caused currency hoarding, which aggravated the short money supply—not that people had a lot to begin with. A farmer in 1770 expected an annual income of about $15 to $30 (about $5000 today), and only if the weather was good. Most were poor, so when the British government began to tax all manner of goods sent to the colonies, including tea, the 13 colonies south of Ontario revolted, fought the American Revolutionary War from 1775 to 1783 and formed a new nation, the U.S.

Tea, coffee, citrus and spices were still in short supply in Ontario after the American war, but, suddenly, into the province came the refugees, the United Empire Loyalists, who left behind a communication network of friends and relatives south of the border. Letters from home arrived containing news of the 13 liberated colonies, which had established new overseas trade links with the same companies that supplied the British traders. The difference was that the Americans' products were reasonably priced. The gist of the feeling in Ontario was, "Send us some of your goods because everything is frightfully expensive here."

Within a few months of letters being sent off, goods started to arrive by whatever conveyance was headed north. Crates of treasured items such as oranges, lemons, limes, tea, coffee, spices and the odd crock of Boston rum were sent at a most reasonable cost. The U.S.-to-Canada crates were so pervasive that they prompted the British Board of Trade in London, England, to recommend to the English Parliament that the Upper Canada legislature be amended to regulate inland trade with the Americans. Customs laws were passed, and tax collectors were stationed at border crossings. Yet, British traders of the time complained that business was still dropping into the red. Well, that was because the mother country had driven people in Ontario to smuggling, by boat. It wasn't until the Customs Consolidation Act of 1841, and then the Canada Customs Act of 1847, that the country began to actively pursue smugglers on both land and water. That was too late for Ontario, though, because avoiding customs and smuggling goods had already become a way of life for many.

Most farmers belonging to buying clubs, which pooled hard currency, sent a few members off in a boat and, after a few days, received a supply of goods and tea that cost half the price of what the British traders charged. Tea smuggling eventually gave way to liquor bootlegging, and the early 20th century was rife with professional smugglers who were often Great Lakes fishermen setting out to either catch or deliver their "midnight herring."

Wet or Dry

In the early 1800s, Toronto distilled more whiskey than any city in Canada, and by the 1860s, it was the hooch capital of North America. In fact, the city's Gooderham and Worts factory was the largest whiskey distiller in the world. Enter the federal Scott Act of 1878, which allowed petitions to force municipal referendums on the sale of spirits, an action that turned intense when around half of Ontario's counties voted to go dry. This experiment in prohibition failed miserably because illegal liquor stills sprouted up like mushrooms and therefore promoted smuggling networks to the U.S. Luckily, the Scott Act had an escape clause that required its vote to be revisited in three years, and when this happened, every dry county voted wet, and that was the end of prohibition until the passing of the Ontario Temperance Act in 1916.

This law was a federal initiative meant to conserve grain for the World War I effort. Here, again, was another failure, because just about every Ontarian had a living relative who knew how to build an illegal still, and the U.S. was just a ride or sail away. After the end of the war, the Temperance Act was supported, but that only served to spur Ontario distilleries to ramp up their production, and, by 1920, by which time the American Congress had passed the Volstead Act that began its great prohibition experiment, Ontario was operating at full throttle. The American Prohibition was, not surprisingly, a dismal failure, but it also sent Ontario's whiskey industry into maximum overdrive, turning distillers into millionaires and vastly improving the lives of grain farmers and fishermen.

The Liquor Men

"Bronfman" means "liquor man" in Yiddish, and when the U.S. passed the prohibition Volstead Act in 1919, Canadian brothers Sam and Harry Bronfman decided to become big-time liquor men, a choice that eventually made them synonymous with smuggling. The Bronfmans, however, never broke the law because even though prohibition existed in Canada, unlike what was outlined in the American Volstead

Act, Canada never actually banned the manufacture of spirits. People were allowed to make and bottle whiskey, but it
had to be sold outside the country. For that, the Bronfman
brothers were well equipped. After they left the family business, a hotel and moonshine operation in Manitoba, in 1916,
and moved east to Montréal, they built stills and became regular distributors of moonshine whiskey. When the Volstead
Act was passed, the brothers built a small distillery in
Saskatchewan that they called the Canada Pure Drug
Company, a name meant to circumvent a regulation in
Ottawa's prohibition legislation that called whiskey a drug.
Sales were slow at first, but when word that two Jewish
brothers from Canada were making top-quality hooch
reached a certain person in the U.S., that person came
calling. Meyer Lansky, a kingpin in New York City's Jewish
Mafia, told Sam, "We'll take all the booze you can ship.
All you gotta do is get it over the border. We'll take it from
there." This wasn't tough, because all the Bronfmans had to
do was fill up a ship, make the declaration to customs that
the whiskey was destined for Europe or South America and
send the ship across the St. Lawrence River.

Anyone who was capable of causing trouble in these
cross-border transactions was either paid off or permanently
removed by Lansky's infamous Murder Incorporated gang.
The whole system worked like a dream, and in 1924, the
Bronfmans built a larger distillery in Montréal that they
called the Distillers Company Limited, after the world's
largest distributor of Scotch whiskey, the Distillers Company
Limited of Edinburgh, Scotland. Ever the salesman, Sam
began cultivating new U.S. customers such as Arnold
Rothstein, "Waxy" Gordon, "Big Maxie" Greenberg and
a host of other East Coast mob bosses. Indeed, whiskey
money was everywhere, and to avoid an embarrassment of
riches that left behind paper trails as evidence of money

laundering, Sam had his mob money deposited in the Bank of Montréal under the name J. Norton. The money was then transferred to foreign banks.

After a few years of this, the U.S. got serious about the interdiction of liquor, so when the St. Lawrence River became too hot for smuggling, Sam looked to Lake Erie. It was a much safer channel, but its best area, the Detroit River, was already staked out by the Bronfmans' main connection, the Seagram Company Ltd. (whose U.S. connection was Chicago mob boss Al Capone). Not wanting to create friction with Capone, Sam and Rothstein bought isolated properties in Maine, where they could unload their ships on lonely beaches and effectively avoid U.S. customs. This venture was successful, and the demand grew, as well as the desire for shipments to come in faster. Small, quick speed-boats could get across the lake in less than an hour, but if the Bronfmans chose this method of transportation, it would mean breaking the law, something they were loath to do. The speedboats were going to have to come from the American side, but were only going to be able to travel halfway across the water, so as not to cross the border. Fishermen were the solution, because if Sam could get them to take his shipments halfway across on the Canadian side, the Americans could pick them up in their speedboats. What Sam did was employ a flotilla of fishing boats that carried the whiskey packed in burlap bags rather than the more obvious crates. There were 50 bottles to a bag, and each bag was attached to a float. The bags came from the distillery by railcar, and so many cars arrived at the lake's ports that locals began calling Lake Erie the "Jewish Lake."

In 1926, the Bronfmans struck a distribution deal with their company's namesake, the Distillers Company in Scotland. It was an arrangement that suited the U.S. mobs to a T—so much so that in 1927, with a nod from Capone, the Bronfmans bought Seagram Company Ltd. and ratcheted up their whiskey production, sending 500,000 bottles across the Detroit River in a year. Between 1927 and the Volstead Act's repeal in 1933, the brothers Bronfman shipped millions of bottles of whiskey to the mobs. About 85 percent was smuggled across the river to Rothstein's hometown of Detroit, and the remainder made the Lake Erie trip in the boats of the midnight herring fishermen.

In 1933, when the Volstead Act was repealed, the Bronfmans continued to make fine whiskey, as well as diversify into other business avenues—oil, food products and real estate. In 1967, Sam was made a Companion of the Order of Canada for the philanthropic use of his bootleg billions.

This was, perhaps, a bit of a stretch, but what the heck, those were adventurous times.

And for curiosity's sake, it's interesting to note that while some of Sam's mob kingpins south of the border were bumped off or went down for the legal count, others such as Lansky escaped immediate prosecution and wisely invested in a desert town called Las Vegas. During the 1980s, all that bootlegger money had a reunification of sorts when Rothstein's son, Murray, who had changed his name to Sumner Redstone, and Sam Bronfman's grandson, Edgar Jr., each bought a large segment of the U.S. entertainment business, with Redstone purchasing Viacom and Edgar buying out MCA/Universal. More than a few of their movies have since featured plots from the days of rum-running, mobs and midnight rides.

Land
O' Immigrants

All over the world money is in flight. People have scraped the world clean...and now they want to run...Koreans, Filipinos, people from Hong Kong and Taiwan, South Africans, Italians, South Americans, Argentines, Colombians, Venezuelans, Bolivians, a lot of black people...Chinese from everywhere...since Switzerland closed down, they are going to the United States and Canada... Toronto, Vancouver, California...Miami.

–V.S. Naipaul, author

SETTLER STORIES

Welcome to Ontario

Ontario has been in the immigration business since its creation as a province in 1867—immigration was, after all, a necessary endeavour for such a large section of Canada that was essentially empty. From the late 1860s to the 1920s, "Come west, young man, for we have endless land and financial opportunities," was the political mantra being spread in Europe. The province is still selling itself in modern times but has since dropped "endless land" from its promotional pitches. New immigrants to Ontario are not interested in endless land—most have done their homework, and they know that almost everyone in the province lives within 160 kilometres of the U.S. border and that the idea of "endless land" is bunk. What's happening, instead, is that billions of dollars are being spent by the Ontario Provincial Nominee Program (PNP) to buy Ontarians out of their familiar city neighbourhoods and allow the construction of luxury condominiums where PNP fast-tracked immigrants can live. Other immigrants, especially refugee claimants, create huge strains elsewhere, such as on municipal treasuries and provincial social programs. Ontario's major cities are bulging with new immigrants, public infrastructures are collapsing, roads are gridlocked, social programs are disintegrating, schools have become gang turfs, police services are overwhelmed, law courts can't find qualified interpreters, and Ontario is still selling itself? It's true that all of these problems can't be exclusively blamed on immigrants, but common sense still dictates a moratorium on immigration to Ontario.

The Annual Tractor Bash

Every year, more than 5000 seasonal farm workers from Mexico and the Caribbean arrive in the Niagara region to harvest the area's bountiful produce. The foreign workers pick and pack fruit and vegetables, do greenhouse labour and help with general farming chores—a duty that usually includes driving a tractor on public highways. In Ontario, a driver's licence isn't required to drive agricultural equipment from one place to another over public roads. Fine, but if a driver hails from a less industrialized country, he or she might not have much driving experience—if any—and is essentially an accident waiting to happen. Hundreds of these tractor-related accidents happen every year.

A Frightful Equation

The 2005 Canada-Ontario Immigration Agreement annually funnels around $250 million federal tax dollars into a massive Ontario people-importing industry. What was once a well-oiled federal government immigrant-selection system based on skills, education and language competency has degenerated into what seems to be a tidal wave of blood relations, refugees and government-visa immigrants, with only about 17 percent going through the formal selection process. Immigration to Ontario has become an industry that employs thousands of consultants, lawyers and social workers, but if immigration here is going to continue, the industry that really needs an injection is home construction. In 2010, Ontario took in approximately 125,000 legal immigrants, 50,000 illegal immigrants and 25,000 refugees, but housing starts in the province for 2010 were barely 49,000 and unemployment was nine percent. Where are the immigrants and refugees going to live? Do MPPs expect them to pile into multi-family apartments? What is the thought process?

The People Squeeze

Southern Ontario has long been a prime destination for immigrants. During the 18th century, they arrived mostly from Britain and settled in the Great Lakes area. One century later, immigration from the entire UK shrunk to 40 percent, with the remaining 60 percent of Ontario immigrants hailing mostly from western Europe. In total, during the 18th and 19th centuries, about 22,000 immigrants arrived in the province annually, which is not an astounding figure, considering that many of the non-British headed for the largely French Canadian–populated northern areas of Ontario. Everyone lived in relative peace until the 20th century, when large numbers of Eastern Europeans and Chinese from BC arrived, and racial prejudice raised its ugly head. These new immigrants discovered southern Ontario closed to any opportunity, save manual labour and shopkeeping. Skilled immigrants were denied professional and union memberships, police services closed ranks and voting rights were denied. Entertainment venues and taverns shut their doors, and even cars and trucks were difficult to procure because in order to obtain a licence, proof of citizenship had to be presented, and this was not an easy document for immigrants to obtain. An immigrant buying or selling property was also rare because most municipalities stated the following covenant of use in land transfers: "None of the lands described herein shall be used or occupied, let or sold to Negroes, or Asiatics, Bulgarians, Austrians, Russians, Serbs, Romanians, Turks, weather [sic] British subjects or not, or foreign born Italians, Greeks, or Jews."

That law lays out pretty clearly how southern Ontario treated immigrants of the early 20th century—they were tolerated (barely), and there was hope that they would be driven away. Only they weren't, and by the end of World War II, when a diverse cross-section of immigrants began arriving in southern Ontario in greater numbers than ever before, the overt bigotry of the past slowly faded along with the ethnic predominance of British Canadians. By 1971, one in four Ontarians was neither British nor French, and in the 1980s and early 1990s, Asian immigration actually made British Canadians a minority in Toronto.

Fast-forward to 2005, when the Places to Grow Act was passed. It essentially "makes room" for upward of 150,000 new immigrant arrivals per year. Overpopulation of the province's metropolitan areas that's caused, in part, by this is prompting Ontario residents to move into the smaller urban enclaves of Lake Ontario's eastern shore, otherwise known as the Golden Horseshoe, the fastest growing urban region in North America. Already home to seven million people, the area's population is expected to surpass 11 million by the year 2030. One of the problems is that most of the Golden Horseshoe is part of Ontario's Greenbelt agricultural land and is therefore out of bounds for developers. The intensification of the area's cities is the government fix, and in the spirit of the Places to Grow Act, provincial authorities have been working with Golden Horseshoe municipal officials to rework smaller town and city infrastructures in the hope of handling the expected influx of people. How residents will react to eventually having to build upward is anyone's guess—maybe everyone will just move out to the country and open boutique wineries. But wait. So many have done that already that the Greenbelt's countryside is looking more like France than Ontario every year. Guess that means Florida is the only other option....

An Odious Incident

The German Pioneers Days Act of 2000 was legislation put in place to honour the 18th-century German immigrants who settled in the Grand River area of the Waterloo Township. In 1833, the mostly German-speaking settlement, then called Sand Hills, was renamed Berlin, after the capital of Germany. In 1912, Berlin was incorporated as a city, but four years later, World War I caused the Ontario government to pressure Berlin's town council to change the town's name to Kitchener, after the British secretary of state for war, Lord Horatio Herbert Kitchener, who went down with his ship that same year, 1916. A name-change referendum was boycotted by incensed Ontarians of German descent, but the government won. Now, however, according to the German Pioneers Days legislation, the first day after Thanksgiving will forever be a day of remembrance for Kitchener residents who have a German heritage. Also celebrated in Kitchener at this time of year is the largest Oktoberfest outside Germany. Residents can don their lederhosen, eat wurst, drink beer and, for a few days, yell out to the world, *"Ich bin ein Berliner!"* No, wait, that's what John F. Kennedy said to the West Berlin crowds during a 1963 Berlin Wall ceremony. It was said that Kennedy's American accent translated the phrase into "I am a jelly doughnut." An urban legend, to be sure, but in order to avoid any semblance of Kennedy's faux pas, Oktoberfest revellers are advised to best leave off the *ein* for a truer interpretation of the phrase.

No Laundries for the Chinese

In 1902, a Toronto bylaw was created to regulate laundry companies and oversee their inspection. Toronto police took on the task of licensing laundries with the express purpose of excluding the Chinese. The Chinese were having a tough go of it in Ontario at this time. Originally recruited to work on the railway in BC, some 17,000 mostly male Chinese individuals were without employment after the completion of the project. While some returned home to China, many drifted east to open restaurants, food markets and laundries. The public's animosity toward these Chinese-run laundries was because of the fear of disease, rather than racism. Chinese laundry workers sprayed water from their mouths when ironing clothes, and when a newspaper reporter alluded to this habit as the cause of the spread of cholera, people freaked out. The truth was that only a few laundry workers spit water on their ironing, but all got tarred with the same brush. "Chink Laundries Cause Disease" was an occasional headline in Ontario newspapers well into the 1930s.

Odds
and Ends

Leave the beaten track occasionally and dive into the woods. Every time you do you will be certain to find something you have never seen before.

–Alexander Graham Bell, scientist and inventor

GOVERNMENT

The Right to Vote

The Parliamentary Elections Act of 1868 gave residents of Ontario the right to vote, as long as they were male British subjects over the age of 21 and owned, rented or occupied real estate worth at least $400 in a city, $300 in a town and $200 in a village or township.

Private and Confidential
The Ontario Municipal Freedom of Information and Protection of Privacy Act safeguards citizens from the release of personal information that has been submitted to governments and institutions. It allows the release of

collected non-personal information, but several circumstances are listed that permit the act to be ignored. The exceptions include national defence investigations, police investigations and the odd possibility that there is a threat to endangered fish or wildlife.

Accosting Accommodators

The Ontario Innkeepers Act of 1990 is a revised provincial statute that allows for automatic liens on the property and livestock of hotel or motel guests up to an amount necessary to cover the costs of lodging and food. Travellers who are on the verge of bankruptcy might want to avoid taking along the family pet as well, because Ontario innkeepers also have lawful grounds to seize and sell off a pet at an auction after 30 days if a debt isn't paid. To avoid dabbling in the auction business, modern-day hotel managers usually reserve rooms on a guest's credit card to secure the repayment of a debt.

Slippery Slope

The Occupiers' Liability Act often provides a wintertime financial bonanza for Ontario lawyers, because most lawsuits brought forward under this provincial legislation are concerned with slips and falls on icy surfaces. In Ontario, it is an occupier's responsibility after a snowfall to immediately clear snow and ice from a property's walkways and stairs. Failure to do so creates a legal liability in the case of an accident. Homeowners can limit their liability by emulating big-box stores and malls by contracting out snow and ice removal, thereby apportioning some of the blame to the contractor. There's also some relief for property owners in the knowledge that under the act, the court has the ability to assign blame to the victim if that person wasn't wearing appropriate footwear for icy conditions. Slipping and breaking a bone can be at least half the victim's fault if that person was, say, wearing flip-flops; women wearing high heels during a fall should probably not even contemplate suing.

Dog Dependability

Also listed under the Occupiers' Liability Act is that fact that an occupier is responsible for the actions of any dogs kept on the premises and is liable for damages caused by attacks or bites. However, if the attack occurs during a break-in, an occupier is excused liability—that is, unless the keeping of the dog is unreasonable for the protection of the persons or property. What this can mean is that residents might find themselves the subject of a lawsuit should their specially trained guard dog ravage the neighbour's kid for taking a shortcut through the yard.

Truth and Fiction

The Good Government Act of 2009 is a repeal and update by the Ontario legislature of more than 300 provincial statutes. It also puts to rest Ontario's long history of Christianity in the law—the act allows testimonies to be valid, even if they're unsupported by oath. In other words, Ontario courts now accept personal assurances of the truth, but liars shouldn't expect to get off lightly, should their words prove false.

Accountable Actions
In 2002, Ontario's legislature created the position of integrity commissioner to oversee the expenses of MPPs and maintain their ethical standards of behaviour. It was hinted that certain cities known to have spendthrift councillors should follow suit. Which cities took the hint? Well, in 2004, Toronto established an office for its own integrity commissioner, and in 2008, in response to less-than-ethical behaviour from some of its councillors, Hamilton city council proposed a bylaw that provided for the appointment of an integrity commissioner. It took some time to pass, but Hamilton got its bylaw in 2010.

Justice is Served

In Ontario, a justice of the peace (JP) doesn't have to be a lawyer or have any training in jurisprudence. To be a JP, candidates are required to be involved in community affairs, have no criminal convictions and be free of pomposity and legal problems such as bankruptcy.

Highland Heritage

The Tartan Act of 2000 is legislation that sanctioned the adoption of a Scottish tartan for Ontario. The tartan has four blocks of colour—green to denote the forests of Ontario, red to represent First Nations bands, blue to recall the provincial waters and white to symbolize the sky. MPPs ought to wear our tartan on a kilt. It might go a long way toward improving their image on the Queen's Park webcast. Not one of them makes less than $100,000, so why do they have to dress so slovenly?

Salt Stains

Road salt is a toxic substance, but its use is exempt under Regulation 339 of the Ontario Environmental Protection Act. Ontario dumps almost three million tonnes of salt into the environment annually, which causes damage to wildlife and plants, and contaminates municipal water sources. The Ontario government claims that cost is the prime reason for road salting (because it's much cheaper than its substitutes), but that seems like simplistic short-term reasoning that ignores the estimated annual $3 billion in damages that are caused by the salt-affected corrosion of Ontario's public infrastructure such as roads and bridges.

Top Tips
Bill 81, the Elimination of Automatic Tips Act of 2010, prohibits the addition of automatic service charges or tips on

restaurant cheques. This legislation is a good thing, but that it wasn't created until 2010 is nothing short of weird.

Financial Follies

Thanks to spending by Ontario's most current administration, the province has been dumped into a financial pickle of major proportions. In 2011, the provincial debt topped an astonishing $220 billion. This astounding figure places every man, woman and child in the province in debt to the tune of almost $17,000. Ontarians read about the financial problems of, say, California, but rarely stop to consider that their own province's debt is actually 10 times the size of the Golden State's.

Ontario's finance minister, Dwight Duncan, has promised to begin repairing the damage using various obtuse methods that include freezing the wages of government employees. This will hardly be effectual, considering that 75 percent of these employees are unionized and the other 25 percent will surely be miffed. Yet, Duncan awarded the Ontario Provincial Police a 12 percent raise over three years.

Are the Liberals intent on losing the next provincial election? Perhaps they just want to hand the Conservatives a financial headache and let them find the remedy—not exactly the best way to build up popularity. And what if, horror of horrors, Ontario needs to be bailed out? Ontario represents 35 percent of the Canadian economy, and if the province had to accept bailout money, such an action would have a drastic effect on Canada as a whole. It's disconcerting that all seems to be la-de-da at Queen's Park, and that the spending continues with money that's apparently being pulled out of thin air.

On One Condition…

Both the Conservatives and Liberals have been guilty of over-regulating provincial laws, enacting an average of 700 to 800 regulations annually. This number is staggering, and it affects industry, forcing many people to leave the province to find work elsewhere. Additionally, according to the Fraser Institute, over-regulation has cost Ontario's economy around $85 billion.

THE PUBLIC

Rural Rivalry

In 1883, the town of Rat Portage (now Kenora) was the principle settlement of a vast territory claimed by both the provinces of Manitoba and Ontario. Rat Portage had competing town councils, police forces, prosecutors and provincial judges. A west-versus-east mentality ruled the town, and its residents, who were mostly male lumbermen, took to wearing side arms, slinging rifles and frequenting saloons with provincial affinities. Things were increasingly tense in the Rat, and with both provincial authorities expecting shootouts, word arrived that the Ontario government had hurriedly sought a resolution of the impasse from the British Privy Council in Westminster, England. A lot was at stake for Ontario because a decision in Manitoba's favour would drastically reduce Ontario's western territories, as well as transfer vast tracts of valuable forest and mineral strikes into the hands of its rival. Ontario held its metaphorical breath while awaiting the decision, and when it came, Ontario was the victor, and the guns of Rat Portage returned to shooting game, but this time solely for the residents of "New Ontario."

Haunted H₂O

For much of the 1800s, Toronto's fashionable Yorkville area consisted of one street, a brickyard, a tollhouse, a few taverns and houses and one huge cemetery named the Toronto General Burying Grounds. In Toronto, if a family lacked the means to pay for a church burial, the body went to this cemetery at Bloor Street and Avenue Road. However, in 1855, in response to complaints from Yorkville's citizenry and property developers about odd-tasting well water, the Upper Canada legislature ordered that the cemetery be closed and the bodies moved. With the cemetery gone, Yorkville boomed, and by 1880, it had grown into a sizable town. Then, suddenly, the water started to taste funny again. Suspecting that only a few hundred graves had been disinterred, townspeople stopped drinking well water altogether and asked Toronto's council if Yorkville could tap into its water supply. Toronto said no, but offered to annex Yorkville into its own city. Yorkville's council denied the proposition and immediately began construction of a pumping station what would pipe Lake Ontario water into the city. Alas, the new water was off as well. Digging the trenches for piping had disturbed the long-buried corpses, and their ancient juices were trickling into Yorkville's water reservoir. In 1883, Yorkville threw in the towel and, with its tail between its legs, became the first of Toronto's many annexations. Five years later, in 1887, Toronto dug up most of the remaining corpses for reburial, but in modern times, almost every excavation in the area uncovers more grim reminders of a leaky past.

Cremation Credo

Ontario residents wanting to divest themselves of Aunt Clara's ashes can do so on Crown land without a permit, but carrying out this rite on private or municipal property requires permission.

Graveyard Grumble

The Ontario Cemeteries Act of 1992 governs the establishment of cemeteries, mausoleums and crematoriums, and their closings. That's correct, closings. Were people fool enough to believe their dearly departed would rest in peace forever? It's possible that living family members might receive an order for disinterment to make way for a new subdivision. Is nothing sacred?

Flagging Support

Tired of haphazard, sloppy flag-lowering to commemorate departed royalty and sundry others, Fort Erie enacted a bylaw to establish a protocol for the lowering of flags. Now, the flag is only lowered for royalty, former or present-day Governors General, lieutenant-governors, former and present-day prime ministers, former and present-day premiers of Ontario, sitting federal and provincial ministers, firefighters lost in the line of duty and Fort Erie office staff and council members. Hey, why not? It is their town, after all.

Butt Out

Lighting up a cigarette on a beach in Arnprior can net offenders a $195 fine. A bit hypocritical, considering the funds to build and maintain its beaches come from provincial grants sourced through tobacco taxes.

Artful Acclamation

In 1990, the George R. Gardiner Museum of Ceramic Art Act was passed, and it allows this museum its tax-free status and executive makeup. Although not weird, per se, it is historically noteworthy to your author, who, in the early 1970s, sold a 400-piece collection of pre-Columbian artwork to Helen and George Gardiner.

Finicky Fees

Toronto bylaw No. 744-1998 provides for the licensing of trades and retail, and sets that fee. The licensing fee to operate an adult entertainment shop or body-rub parlour is $7000, whereas farmers selling produce at farmers' markets pay $5. Victualling houses, ordinary places where fruit, fish, oysters, clams or provisions are sold to be eaten therein, pay a fee of $183. One can only assume that a "victualling house" is the Edwardian term for restaurant!

Saturday Sales

In Deseronto, a quaint town on the Bay of Quinte, yard sales have always been popular, but in 2008, the entire town had one giant yard sale for everybody. Sensing a unique tourist opportunity, the town council passed a bylaw declaring the second Saturday in September as the official day for the annual Deseronto Yard & Sidewalk Sale.

Smoking Stoppage

Tired of cleaning up cigarette butts inside its town's park, Goderich's council passed a bylaw in 2010 that banned smoking on the property. This is a walk-in-the-park (wink) bylaw that will undoubtedly expand to include other areas of Goderich, which could be a risky action for a tourist destination in a province where 2.3 million people use tobacco products.

Ashes Axiom

Kapuskasing is so against smoking that the town council included a ban against ashtrays in the workplace in its anti-smoking bylaw. "Gee, officer, that's not an ashtray. That's my dog's dinner bowl!"

Nuisance Notice

Georgina, near Lake Simcoe, has a "public nuisance abatement bylaw" that prohibits begging. This bylaw also prohibits three people on a sidewalk, so as not to inhibit the flow of pedestrian traffic. One has to imagine this law refers to three people walking abreast...

Institutional Ignorance

The first Monday in August is a municipal holiday across Ontario, and depending on the community, the day is named after various local historical luminaries. Toronto's honoured personage is John Graves Simcoe, the city founder for whom the city celebrates "Simcoe Day." However, according to a recent poll in Toronto, only 16 percent of residents know who he is, or anything about his province-building involvement.

Committed to Compost

Barrie is so gung-ho on composting waste that it will sell residents a backyard composter at cost, as well as provide free how-to advice courtesy of one of its Master Composters. Let's hope for the sake of local taxpayers that Master Composters double as the dogcatchers.

Sewage Statute

In Huntsville, a new bylaw has been passed requiring that the homes of all residents, cottages of non-residents, septic systems and all privies be examined by the town's sewer inspector. A fee of $40 is charged, and it's good to know that Art Carney's *Honeymooners* character, Ed Lillywhite Norton, is still alive and well, and living in Huntsville.

Merry in Manitoulin

Gore Bay's population is approximately 900, and it's the largest community on Manitoulin Island, as well as a wonderful place to live or visit. Nice people live in Gore Bay, real Ontarians, and they have so few problems that their town only has three bylaws: do not feed the deer, do not hook a driveway onto the highway without a permit and make sure retail businesses have access-ways for the disabled. Bylaw committee members, who are just regular people, also deal with any other community problems.

Innocent Until Proven Guilty

Milton, a farming area in the municipality of Halton, slightly west of Toronto, is such a friendly place that even bylaw offenders are treated in a respectful manner not seen in many other Ontario communities. Milton refers to its scofflaws as "suspected offenders," which is a good and proper attitude that should be plucked off the municipal council grapevine by cities and towns everywhere. Milton is also sensitive to pet owners—its dogcatchers don't ransom off animals, and if a resident's horse escapes from its paddock, the animal will be returned with a smile, not a fine.

Vomit Violation
Beware of errant bodily functions in Niagara Falls. Throwing up on the street contravenes the "nuisance bylaw," as does urinating and spitting, and the kicking of blue boxes. Committing any of these misdemeanours can net an offender a maximum $10,000 fine.

Warrant to Wheel

The town of Smiths Falls is apparently an active recruiter of immigrants, and to make newcomers feel more at home, the town council passed a 2010 bylaw that allows rickshaws to be licensed.

WARS

Water Warfare

The Treaty of Ghent, signed in 1814, is the reason why
Ontario's lake ports never receive visits from foreign warships.
As a way to avoid hostilities on the Great Lakes, Britain and
the U.S. agreed to never allow warships to enter the
St. Lawrence River. The Treaty of Ghent is as much a law
today as it was in 1814, and Ontario is probably all the better
for not having warships prowling its waterways.

Conscription Contention

The Foreign Enlistment Act of 1818 was created by British Parliament, and the act declared it illegal for British subjects to serve in or be recruited into foreign armies. Defying this law, almost 20,000 Ontarians served with either the Union or Confederate forces during the American Civil War. During the years of the war, which lasted from 1861 to 1865, the Ontario cities of Niagara, Toronto and St. Catharines were hotbeds of Confederate activities, with the stylish Queen's Hotel (now the Fairmont Royal York) on Toronto's Front Street serving as unofficial Confederate headquarters for the last years of the conflict.

Patriotic Loyalties

During the American Civil War, on May 14, 1861, a U.S. warship, the *San Jacinto*, almost turned the conflict into a world war when it stopped and boarded the British merchant ship, the *Trent*, taking two Confederate diplomats as its prisoners. The Trent Affair infuriated both Britain and France, and the U.S. received threats of war from both countries. John A. Macdonald's government in Ottawa drafted the Militia Act as a preparatory measure and to provide for conscription, if necessary. Conflict with Britain and France was averted, however, with an apology from the U.S. and the release of the diplomats. Much of Ontario, though, held fast to its American loyalties, and at the war's end, Niagara welcomed many Confederate political and military luminaries into its fold until the victorious Union granted them amnesty. General John C. Breckinridge, the Confederate secretary of war, along with generals Jubal Early, John Hood, Henry Heth and Richard Taylor, were just some of the prominent names to be found in town.

United They Stand

Two years after the American Civil War was over, on May 30, 1867, support for the South was still strong as nearly all of Toronto was on the docks to cheer for and welcome the visiting former Confederate president Jefferson Davis, who credited their continual support, hearty greeting and a local band's playing of "Dixie" for the revival of his spirit and the saving of his life—two years in a U.S. federal prison had taken its toll.

Lincoln, London and a Lieutenant

Also of interest during this period is the assassination of U.S. president Abraham Lincoln, which was a plot partly conceived in Ontario at the Queen's Hotel in 1864, and that was brought to its conclusion by Edward P. Doherty. Born in London, Ontario, Lieutenant Doherty, who was part of the 16th New York Cavalry, fired the fatal shot that killed Lincoln's assassin, John Wilkes Booth, on April 25, 1865.

Conclusion

*A conclusion is the place where
you got tired of thinking.*

−Arthur Bloch, author

THE LAST WORD

As you can see by now, many of Ontario's provincial and municipal laws are, at the very least, weird. This is for a variety of reasons, but even I have to admit that the province's law-makers at both levels of government have tried—and still try—to do a good job by Ontarians. This admission, however, doesn't mean I think *all* is well in Ontario's political chambers. Municipal councils often appear too fixated on generating income, while provincial MPPs seem habitually hamstrung by the tail wagging the dog. Restrictive parameters also often serve as excuses for doing nothing, and although the words "eco" or "green" can spur instant action, existing problems in immigration and multiculturalism are matters that routinely get swept under the table in order to avoid the antagonization of ethnic minorities. Coupled with the apparent infighting for control that rules Queen's Park, the result is disappointment for many Ontarians.

The treasury is stuffed with IOUs, employment is down, social programs are a mess, city infrastructures are crumbling, many consider police services to be predatory and housing is far too expensive. Are these issues that could be remedied at the next election? Maybe, if history hadn't polarized Ontario into, essentially, two political parties, each of which have fiercely dedicated followers who allow for relative predictability at the polls. If you read the newspaper, it's not that difficult to predict an election's results.

Governing for the betterment of government is the worst kind of socialism, and Ontarians need to put some thought into their decisions before casting their ballots. Citizens should vote for good government, not for the good of government, otherwise we all might end up sitting in a park, not allowed to do anything, while wishing we would have done something.

ABOUT THE ILLUSTRATORS

Roger Garcia

Roger Garcia immigrated to Canada from El Salvador at the age of seven. Because of the language barrier, he had to find a way to communicate with other kids. That's when he discovered the art of tracing. It wasn't long before he mastered this highly skilled technique, and by age 14, he was drawing weekly cartoons for the *Edmonton Examiner*. He taught himself to paint and sculpt, and then in high school and college, Roger skipped class to hide in the art room all day in order to further explore his talent. Currently, Roger's work can be seen in a local weekly newspaper and in places around Edmonton.

Peter Tyler

Peter Tyler is a recent graduate of the Vancouver Film School's Visual Art and Design and Classical Animation programs. Though his ultimate passion is in filmmaking, he is also intent on developing his draftsmanship and storytelling, with the aim of using those skills in future filmic misadventures.

Patrick Hénaff

Born in France, Patrick Hénaff is mostly self-taught. He is a versatile artist who has explored a variety of media under many different influences. He now uses primarily pen and ink to draw, and then processes the images on computer. He is particularly interested in the narrative power of pictures.

ABOUT THE ILLUSTRATORS

Djordje Todorovic

Djordje Todorovic is an artist/illustrator living in Toronto, Ontario. He first moved to the city to go to York University to study fine arts. It was there that he got a taste for illustrating while working as the illustrator for his college paper *Mondo Magazine*. He has since worked on various projects and continues to perfect his craft. Aside from his artistic work, Djordje devotes his time to volunteering at the Print and Drawing Centre at the Art Gallery of Ontario. When he is not doing that, he is out trotting the globe.

Roly Wood

Roly Wood has worked in Toronto as a freelance illustrator, and has been employed in the graphic design department of a landscape architecture firm. In 2004, he wrote and illustrated a historical comic book set in Lang Pioneer Village, near Peterborough, Ontario. To see more of Roly's work, visit www.rolywood.com.

Craig Howrie

Craig is a self-taught artist who has known the author for longer than either of them would care to admit. His line art has been used in local businesses' private events as well as a local comic book art anthology. He is also a songwriter working feverishly at a project to see the light of day hopefully within the next decade or so....

ABOUT THE AUTHOR

A.H. Jackson

A.H. Jackson believes that in the twine of life, there are two special genes unique to humankind—hope and humour—and he thinks we should all turn to the funny side of life in the face of adversity. He must have quite the sense of humour, then, since he's been struck by lightning five times!

A prolific writer of non-fiction, Jackson is also a creator of worlds in the fiction realm. This is for children, mostly, because they have imaginations unconstrained by reality. Can pigs fly? No, but in one of his books, a pig talks, plots and saves mankind from becoming the bottom link of the food chain.

Jackson lives in Toronto with a wife named M and a squirrel called Mommy. He is the author of various non-fiction titles, including *Weird Canadian Weather* and *Weird Ontario Weather*, also from Blue Bike Books.